THE BEST CHILDREN'S SONGS EVER

The following songs are the property of:

BOURNE CO.
Music Publishers
5 West 37th Street
New York, NY 10018

Baby Mine
Give a Little Whistle
Heigh-Ho
When You Wish Upon a Star
Whistle While You Work
Who's Afraid of the Big Bad Wolf?

ISBN 978-0-7935-8966-1

HAL•LEONARD®
CORPORATION
7777 W. BLUEMOUND RD. P.O. BOX 13819 MILWAUKEE, WI 53213

Visit Hal Leonard Online at
www.halleonard.com

CONTENTS

ALOUETTE

With spirit, but not too fast

Traditional

The words mean: Little lark, I'm going to pluck your feathers.
I'll pluck your head (la têt')

Each time the chorus is sung, a part of the body is added, as for example
le bec (beak); le nez (nose); les yeux (eyes); le cou (neck) etc.

ALPHABET SONG

Traditional

BABY MINE

Words by NED WASHINGTON
Music by FRANK CHURCHILL

Moderately Slow

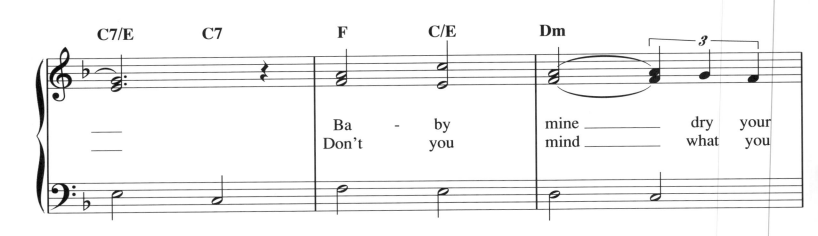

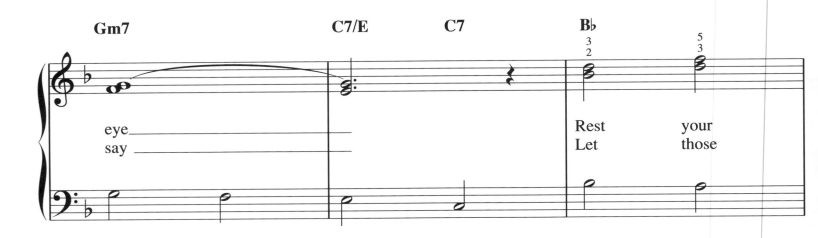

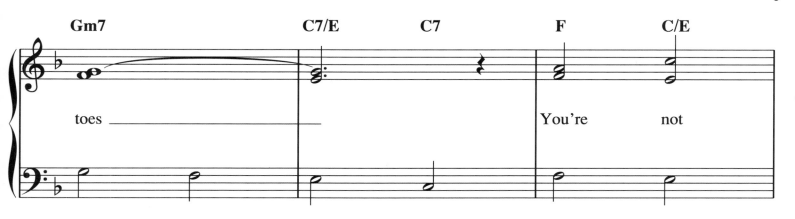

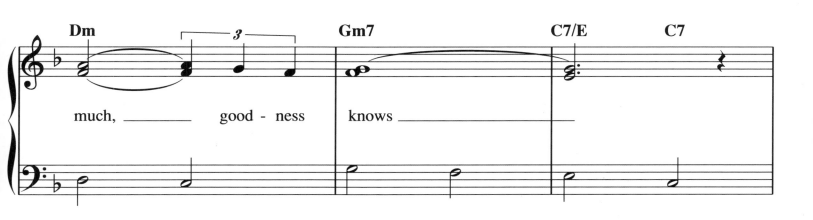

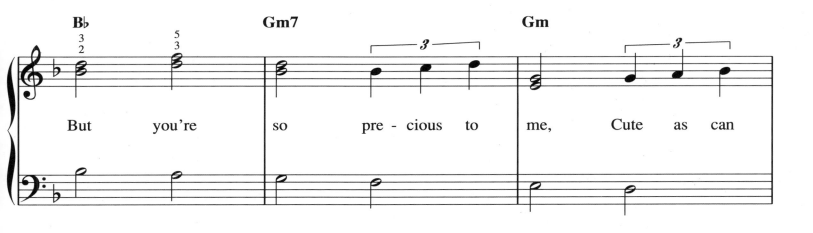

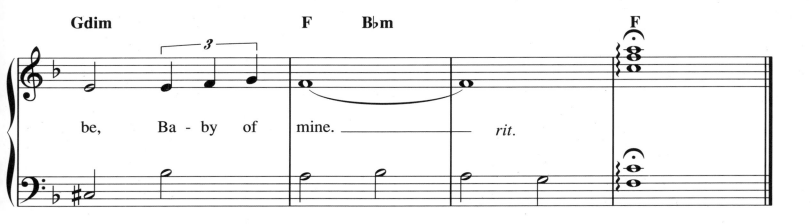

THE BALLAD OF DAVY CROCKETT

from Walt Disney's DAVY CROCKETT

Words by TOM BLACKBURN
Music by GEORGE BRUNS

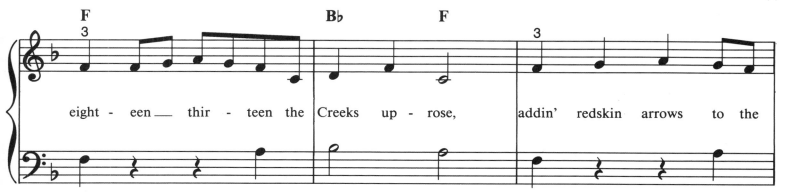

eight - een __ thir - teen the Creeks up - rose, addin' redskin arrows to the

coun - try's __ woes. Now In - jun fight - in' is some - thin' he knows, so he

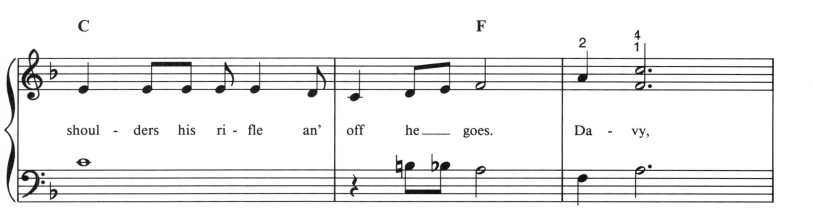

shoul - ders his ri - fle an' off he __ goes. Da - vy,

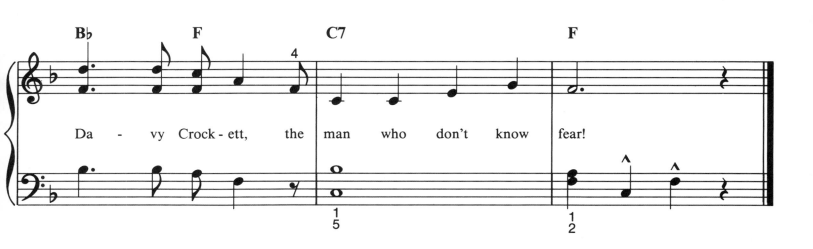

Da - vy Crock - ett, the man who don't know fear!

THE BARE NECESSITIES
from Walt Disney's THE JUNGLE BOOK

Words and Music by
TERRY GILKYSON

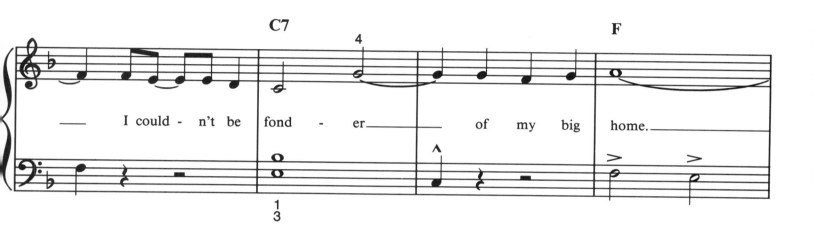

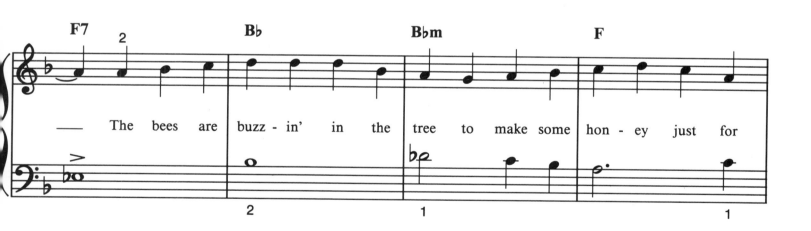

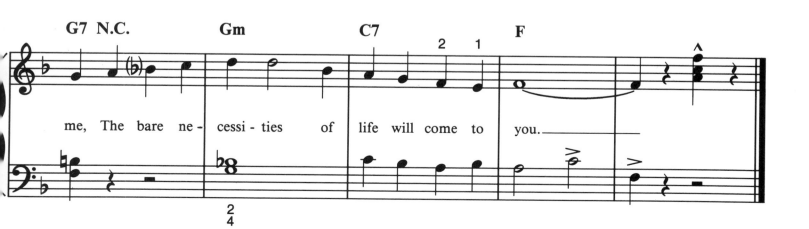

BE KIND TO YOUR PARENTS

from FANNY

Words and Music by
HAROLD ROME

Rhythmic (like a polka)

Be kind to your par – ents, Tho' they don't de – serve it. Re – mem – ber they're grown – ups, A dif – fi – cult stage of

life   They're   apt   to   be   ner - vous   and

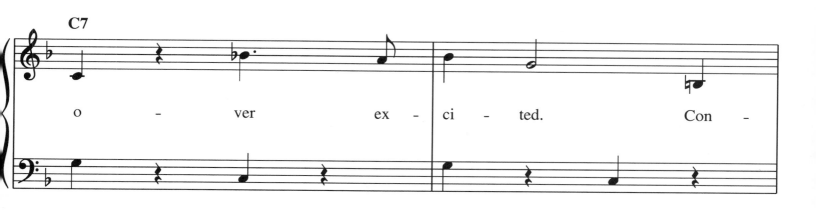

o - ver   ex - ci - ted.   Con -

fused   from   their   dai - ly   storm   and

strife. _____ Just   keep   in   mind, _____

spite of the fool – ish things they do! _____

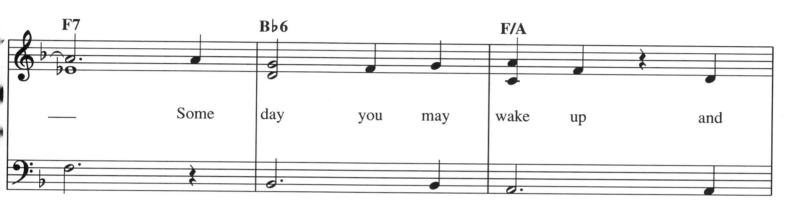

_____ Some day you may wake up and

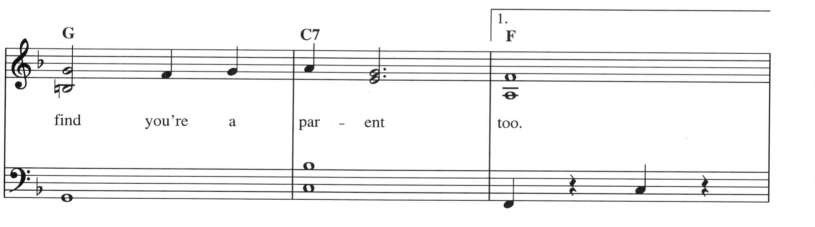

find you're a par – ent too.

1.

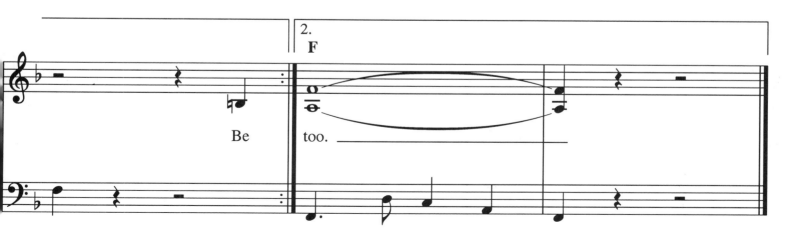

2.

Be too. _____

BEAUTY AND THE BEAST

from Walt Disney's BEAUTY AND THE BEAST

Lyrics by HOWARD ASHMAN
Music by ALAN MENKEN

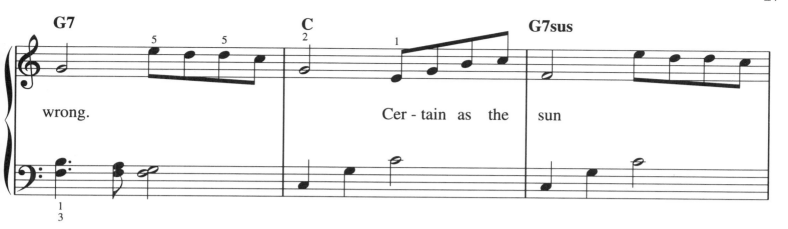

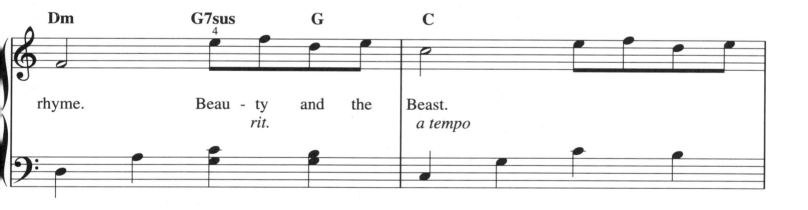

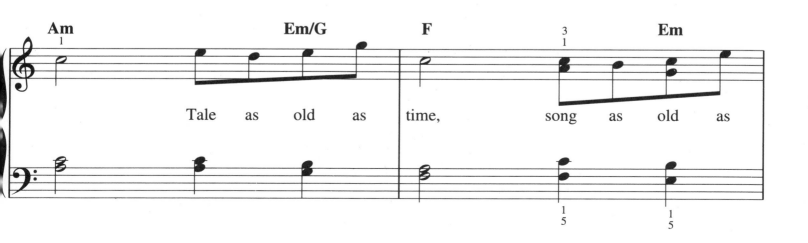

rhyme.   Beau - ty   and   the   Beast.

BIBBIDI-BOBBIDI-BOO
(The Magic Song)
from Walt Disney's CINDERELLA

Words by JERRY LIVINGSTON
Music by MACK DAVID and AL HOFFMAN

Light Schottische

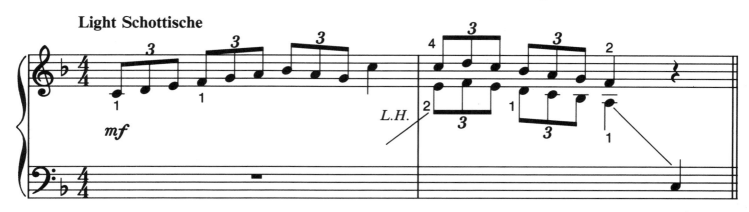

Sa - la - ga - doo - la men - chic - ka boo - la, Bib - bi - di - Bob - bi - di - Boo.

Put 'em to - geth - er and what have you got? Bib - bi - di - Bob - bi - di - Boo.

BINGO

Traditional

THE BLUE TAIL FLY
(Jimmy Crack Corn)

Words and Music by
DANIEL DECATUR EMMETT

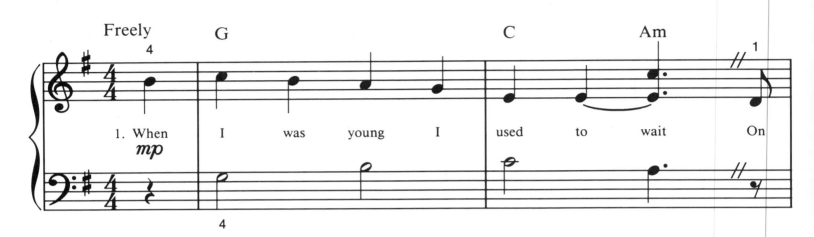

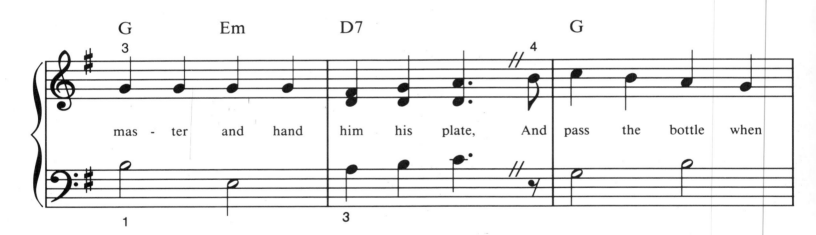

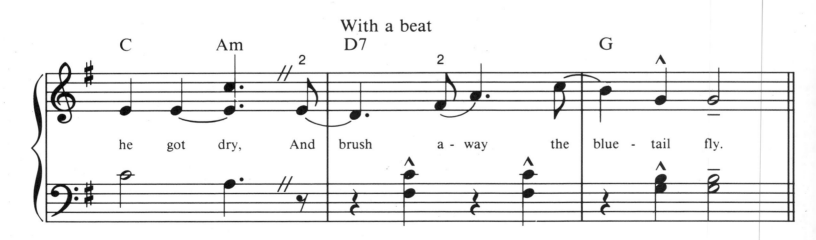

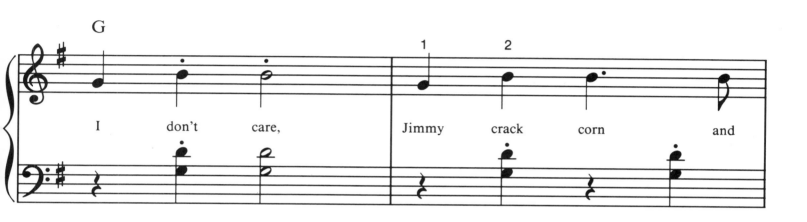

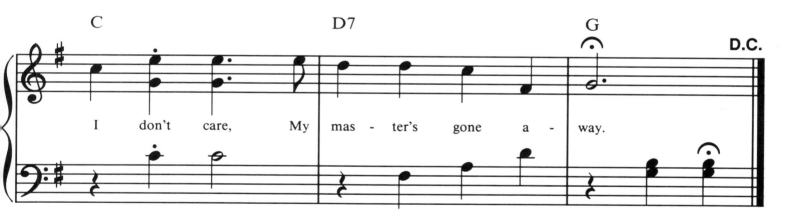

Additional Words

2. And when he'd ride in the afternoon,
   I'd follow after with a hickory broom;
   The pony being like to shy
   When bitten by a blue-tail fly.

3. One day he ride around the farm,
   The flies so numerous, they did swarm.
   One chanced to bite him on the thigh;
   The devil take the blue-tail fly!

4. The pony run, he jump, he pitch;
   He threw my master in the ditch.
   He died — and the jury wondered why —
   The verdict was the blue-tail fly.

5. They laid him under a 'simmon tree;
   His epitaph is there to see:
   "Beneath this stone I'm forced to lie,
   A victim of the blue-tail fly."

THE BRADY BUNCH
Theme from the Paramount Television Series THE BRADY BUNCH

Words and Music by SHERWOOD SCHWARTZ
and FRANK DEVOL

Moderately fast, in 2

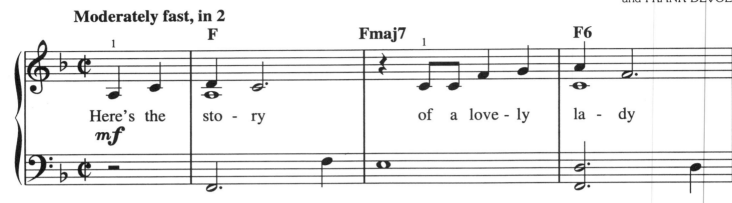

Here's the sto - ry of a love - ly la - dy

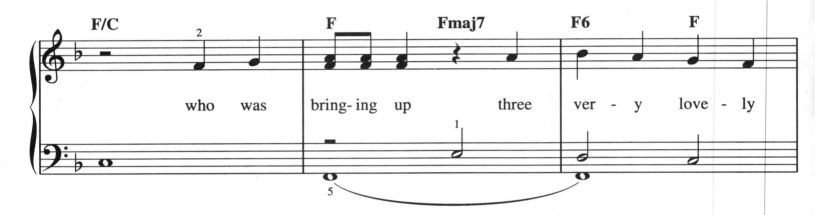

who was bring-ing up three ver - y love - ly

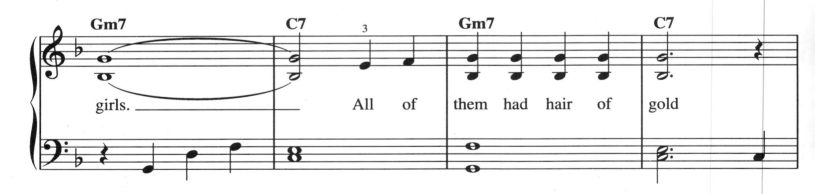

girls. _____ All of them had hair of gold

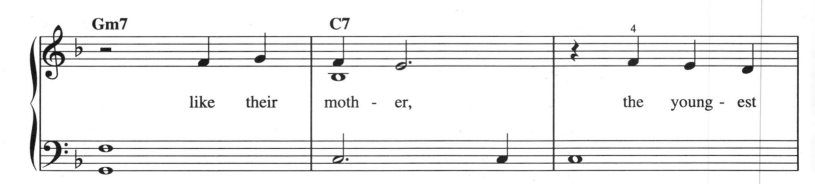

like their moth - er, the young - est

one in curls. It's the sto - ry

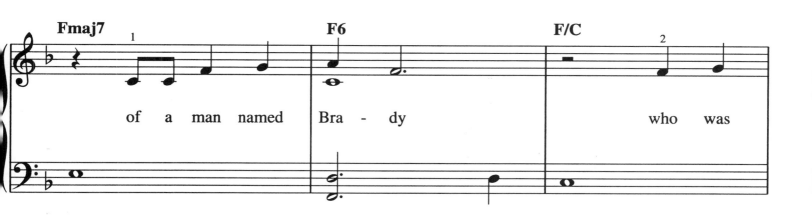

of a man named Bra - dy who was

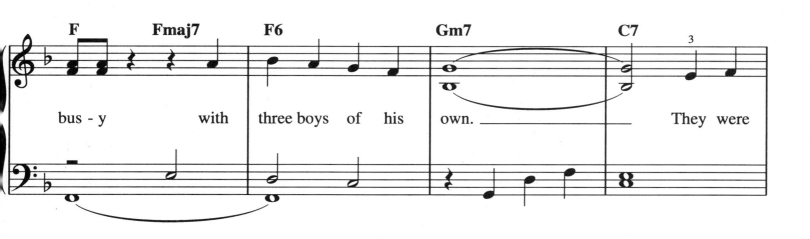

bus - y with three boys of his own. _____ They were

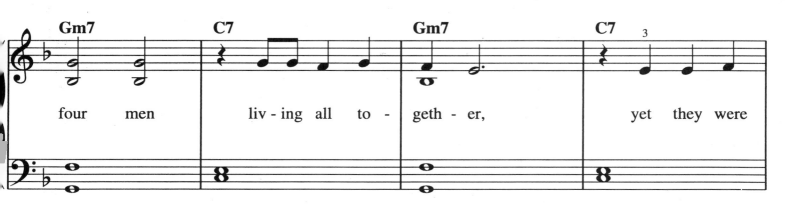

four men liv - ing all to - geth - er, yet they were

33

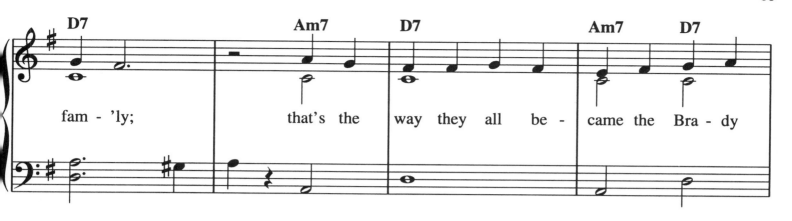

fam - 'ly;   that's the   way they all be -   came the Bra - dy

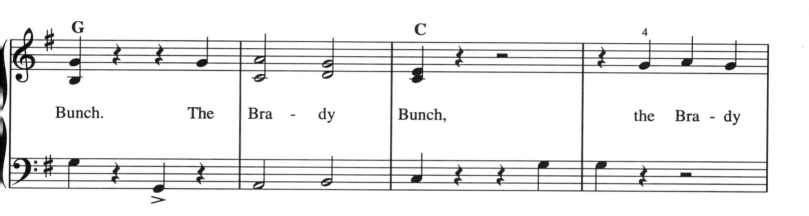

Bunch.   The   Bra - dy   Bunch,   the Bra - dy

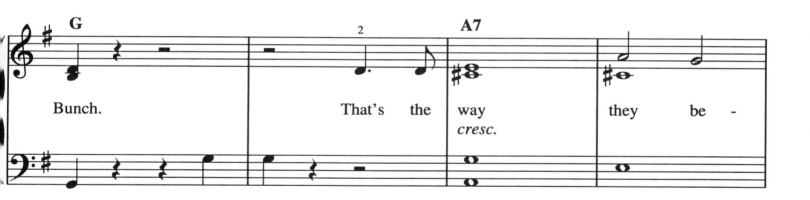

Bunch.   That's the way   they be -

cresc.

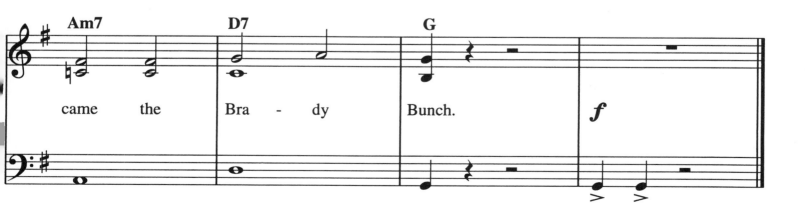

came   the   Bra - dy   Bunch.   ***f***

CANDLE ON THE WATER
from Walt Disney's PETE'S DRAGON

Words and Music by AL KASHA
and JOEL HIRSCHHORN

Slow Spiritual Ballad

I'll be your can - dle on the wa - ter,
I'll be your can - dle on the wa - ter,

My love for you will al - ways burn.
'Til ev - 'ry wave is warm and bright.

I know you're
My soul is

lost and drift - ing,
there be - side you,

But the clouds are lift - ing,
Let this can - dle guide you

don't give up, you have some - where to turn.
soon you'll see a gold - en stream of

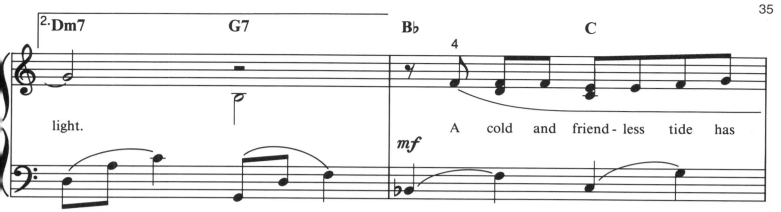

light.

A cold and friend-less tide has

found you,

Don't let the storm-y dark-ness

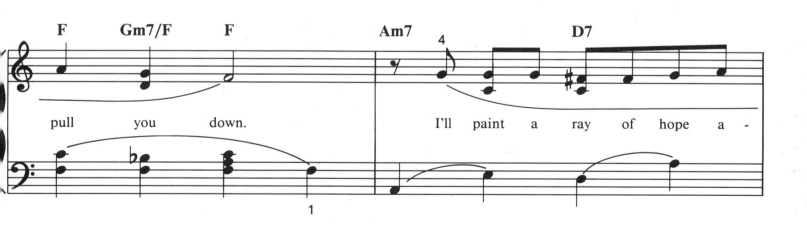

pull you down.

I'll paint a ray of hope a-

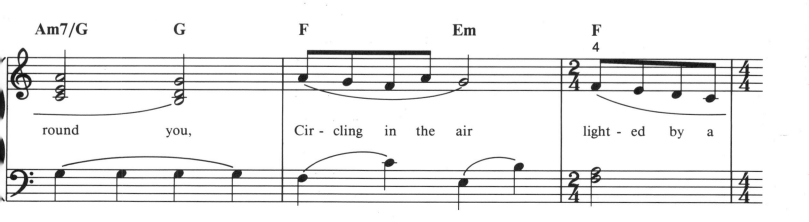

round you,

Cir - cling in the air

light - ed by a

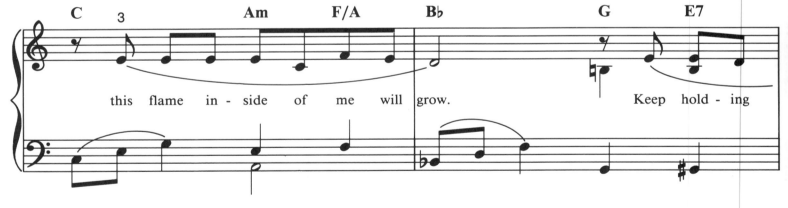

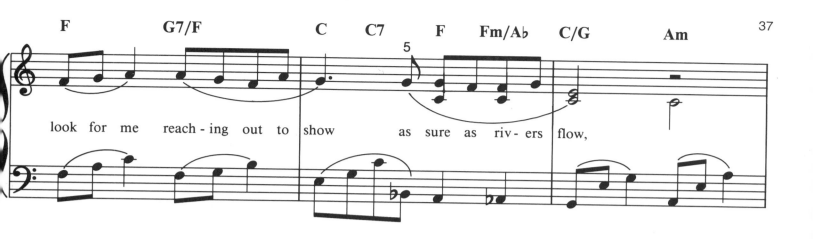

look for me reach-ing out to show as sure as riv-ers flow,

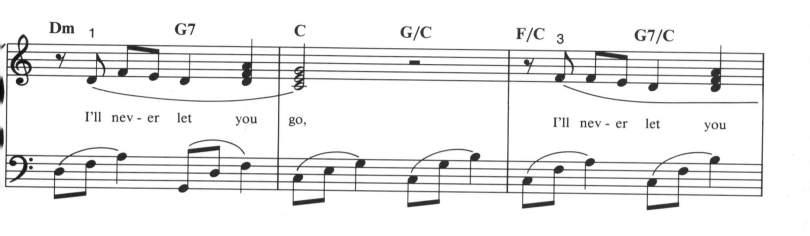

I'll nev-er let you go, I'll nev-er let you

go, I'll nev-er let you go.

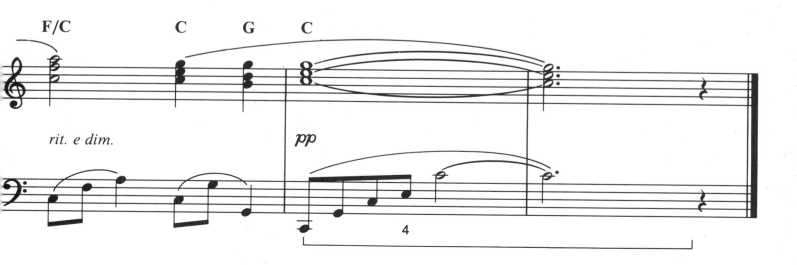

rit. e dim.

pp

THE CANDY MAN

from WILLY WONKA AND THE CHOCOLATE FACTORY

Words and Music by LESLIE BRICUSSE
and ANTHONY NEWLEY

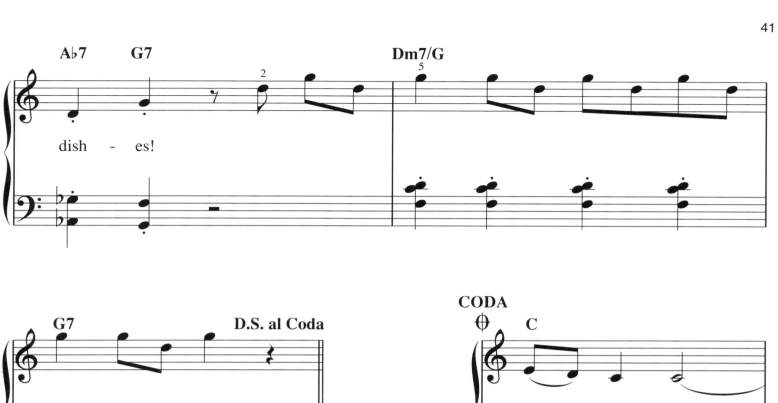

dish - es!

CODA

G7 D.S. al Coda C

world__ taste good. __

Very slowly - freely

Am7   D7   Dm7/G

__ And the world tastes good 'cause the can - dy man thinks__ it

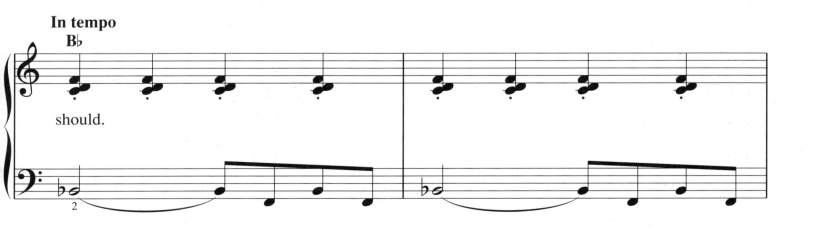

In tempo

B♭

should.

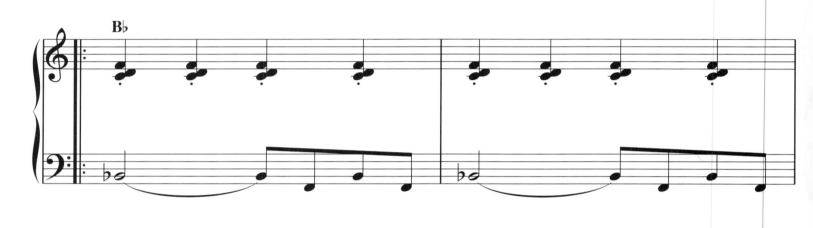

Repeat and Fade

Additional Lyrics

3. Who can take tomorrow, dip it in a dream.
Separate the sorrow and collect up all the cream?
The candy man, the candy man can.
The cany man can 'cause he mixes it with
love and makes the world taste good.

CASPER THE FRIENDLY GHOST

from the Paramount Cartoon

Words by MACK DAVID
Music by JERRY LIVINGSTON

CHIM CHIM CHER-EE

from Walt Disney's MARY POPPINS

Words and Music by RICHARD M. SHERMAN
and ROBERT B. SHERMAN

Lightly, with gusto

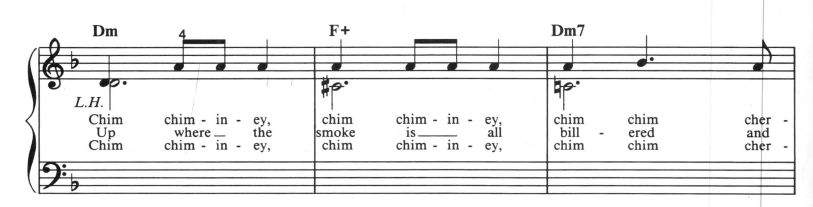

Chim chim-in-ey, chim chim-in-ey, chim chim cher-
Up where __ the smoke is __ all bill- ered and
Chim chim-in-ey, chim chim-in-ey, chim chim cher-

ee! A sweep is as luck- y as
curled 'Tween pave- ment and stars is
ee! When you're with a sweep you're in

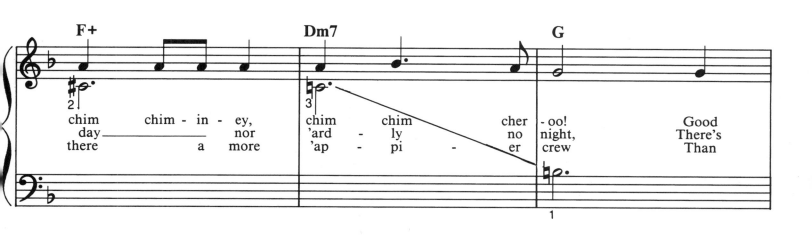

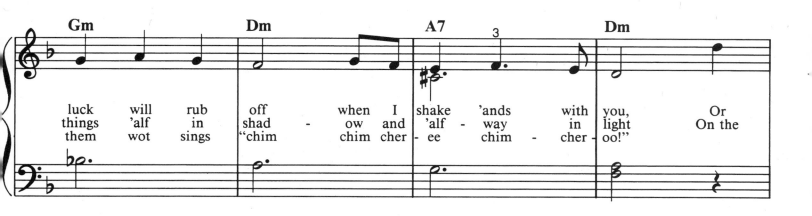

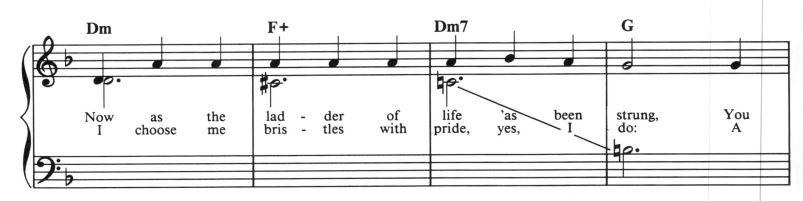

Dm   **F+**   **Dm7**   **G**

Now as the | lad - der of | life 'as been | strung, You
I choose me | bris - tles with | pride, yes, I | do: A

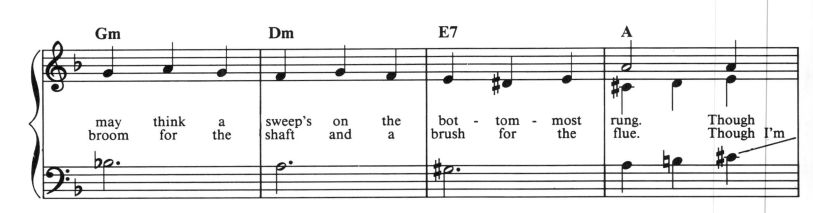

Gm   **Dm**   **E7**   **A**

may think a | sweep's on the | bot - tom - most | rung. Though
broom for the | shaft and a | brush for the | flue. Though I'm

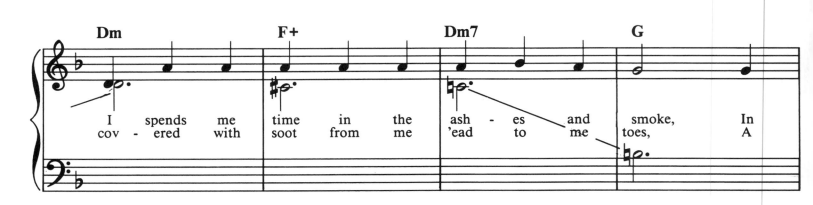

Dm   **F+**   **Dm7**   **G**

I spends me | time in the | ash - es and | smoke, In
cov - ered with | soot from me | 'ead to me | toes, A

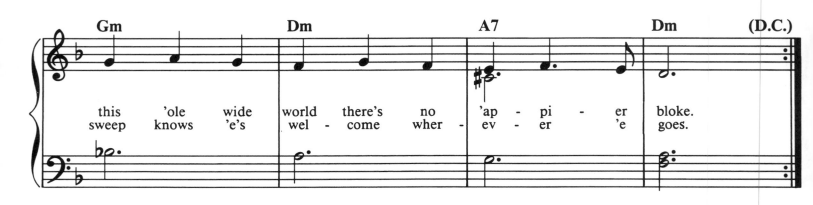

Gm   **Dm**   **A7**   **Dm**   (D.C.)

this 'ole wide | world there's no | 'ap - pi - er | bloke.
sweep knows 'e's | wel - come wher - | ev - er 'e | goes.

DO-RE-MI

from THE SOUND OF MUSIC

Lyrics by OSCAR HAMMERSTEIN II
Music by RICHARD RODGERS

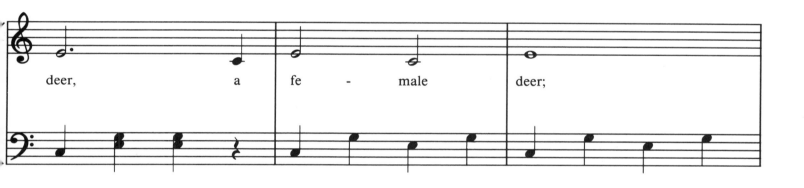

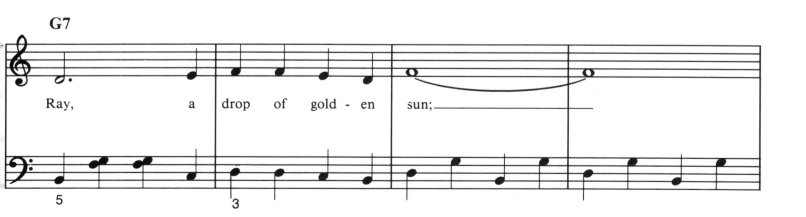

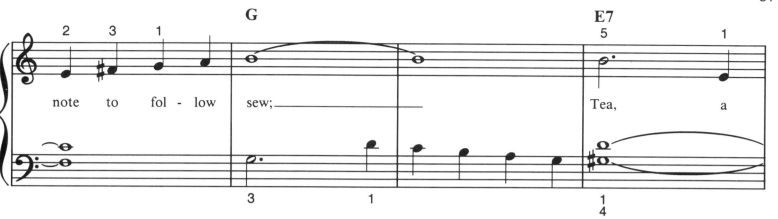

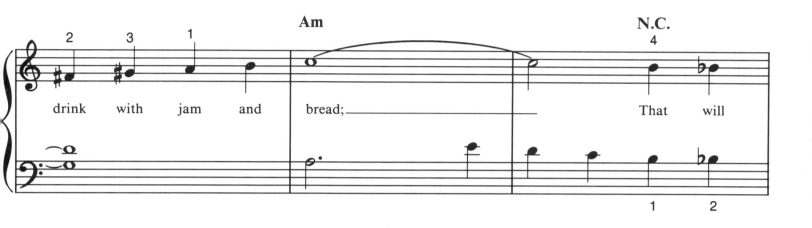

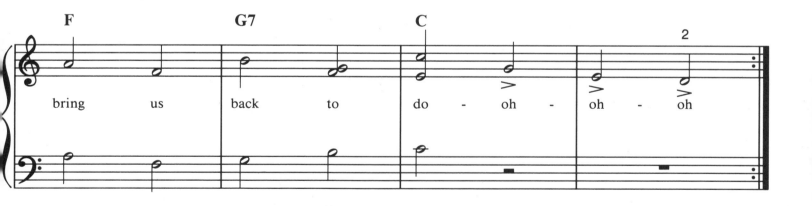

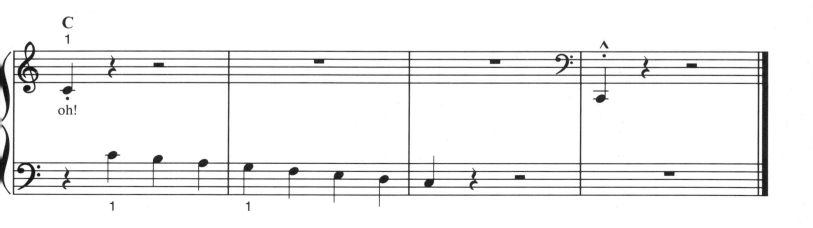

(Oh, My Darling)
CLEMENTINE

Words and Music by
PERCY MONTROSE

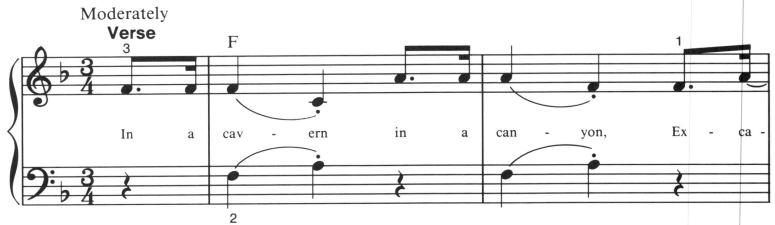

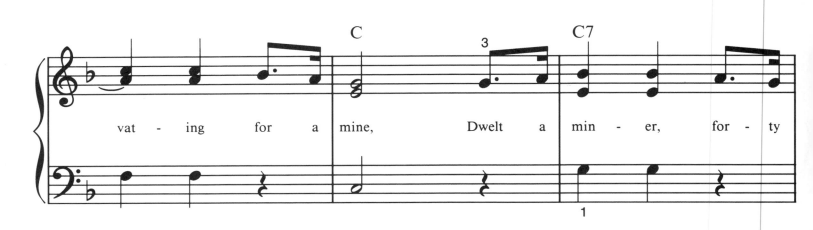

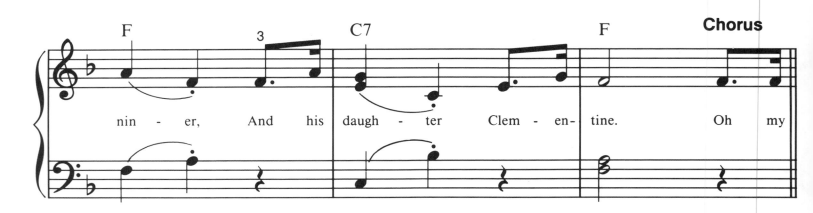

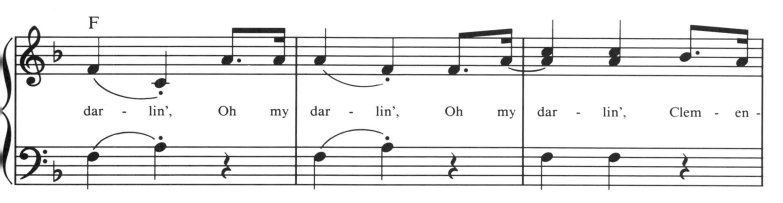

dar - lin', Oh my dar - lin', Oh my dar - lin', Clem - en -

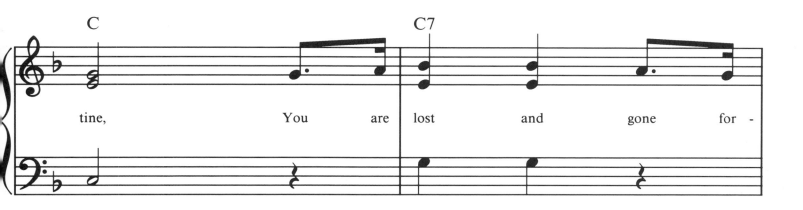

tine, You are lost and gone for -

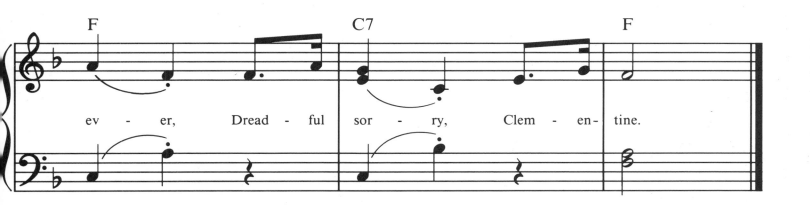

ev - er, Dread - ful sor - ry, Clem - en- tine.

Additional Words

Light she was, and like a fairy, and her shoes were number nine,
Herring boxes without topses, sandals were for Clementine.
(Repeat Chorus)

Drove she ducklings to the water every morning just at nine,
Hit her foot against a splinter, fell into the foaming brine.
(Repeat Chorus)

Ruby lips above the water, blowing bubbles soft and fine,
Alas for me! I was no swimmer, so I lost my Clementine.
(Repeat Chorus)

CRUELLA DE VIL
from Walt Disney's 101 DALMATIANS

Words and Music by
MEL LEVEN

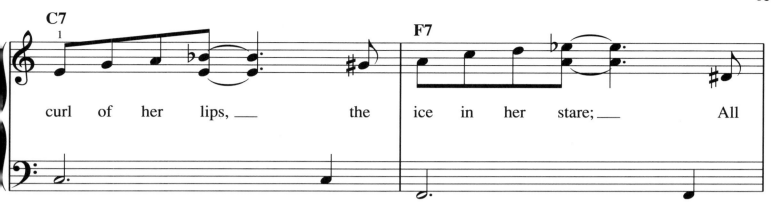

curl of her lips, ___ the ice in her stare; ___ All

in - no - cent chil - dren had bet - ter be - ware. ___ She's

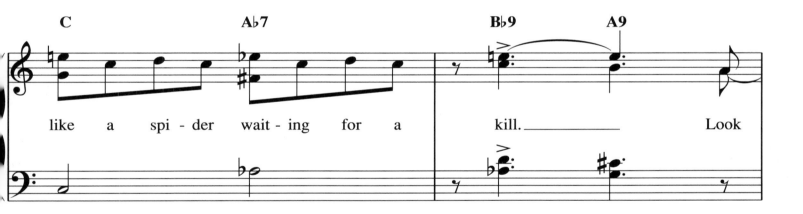

like a spi - der wait - ing for a kill. ___ Look

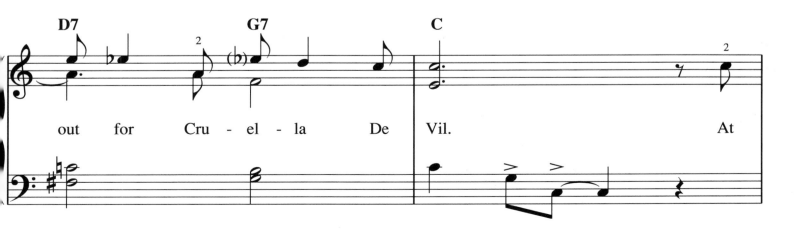

out for Cru - el - la De Vil. At

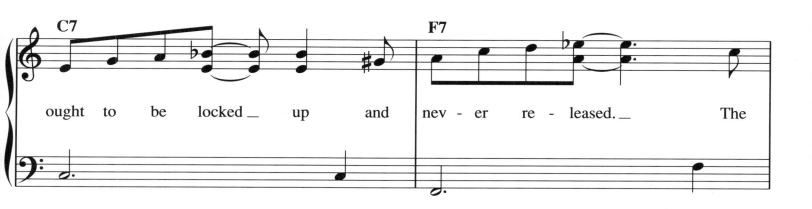

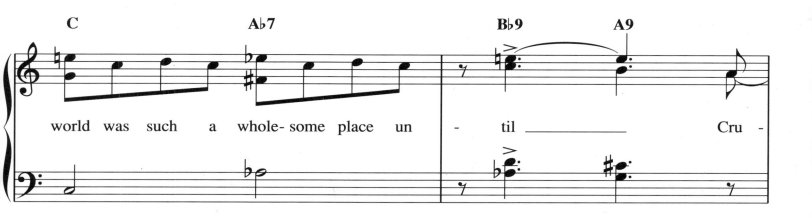

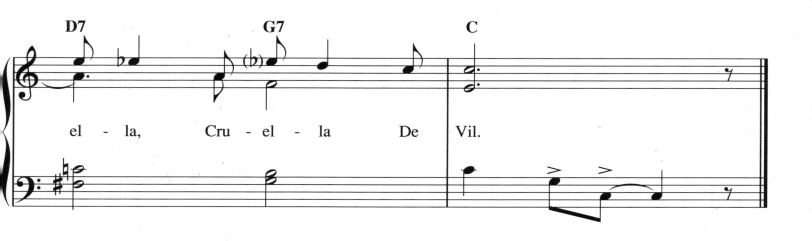

DITES-MOI
(Tell Me Why)
from SOUTH PACIFIC

Lyrics by OSCAR HAMMERSTEIN II
Music by RICHARD RODGERS

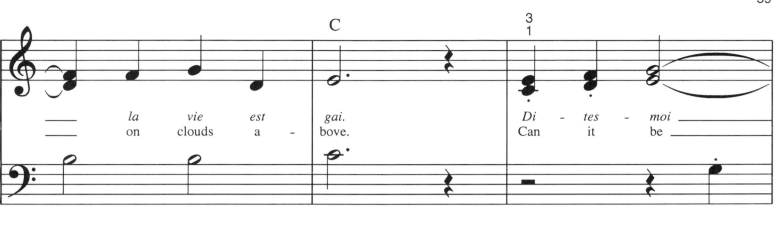

la vie est gai. / on clouds a - bove.
Di - tes - moi / Can it be

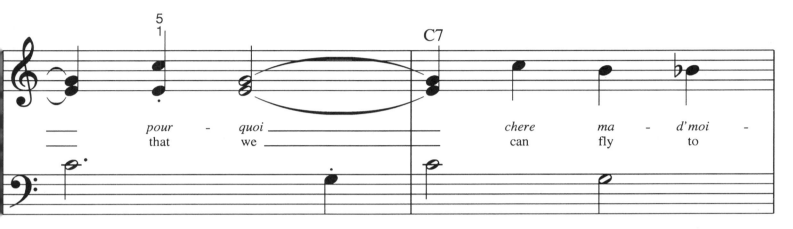

pour - quoi / that we
chere ma d'moi - / can fly to

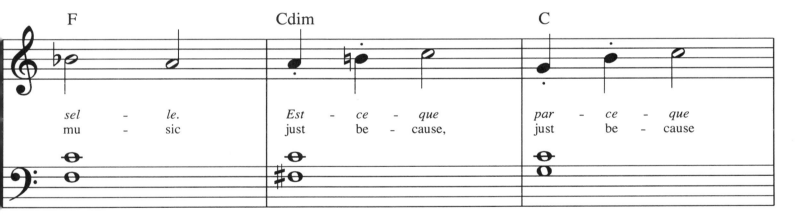

sel - le. / mu - sic
Est - ce - que / just be - cause,
par - ce - que / just be - cause

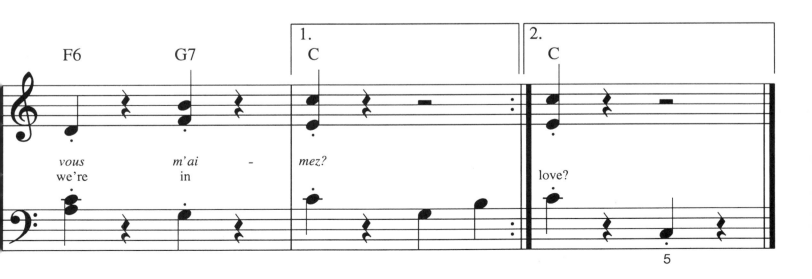

vous m'ai - / we're in
1. mez?
2. love?

DOWN BY THE STATION

Traditional

61

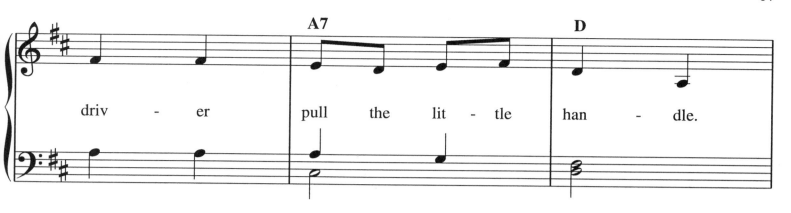

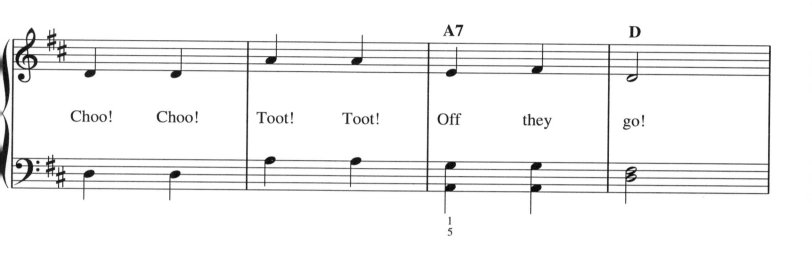

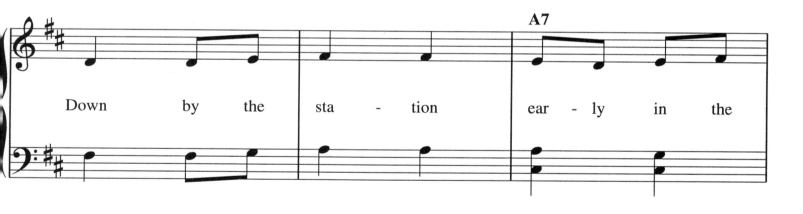

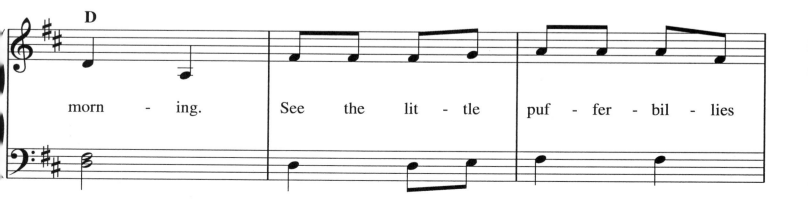

DOWN IN MY HEART

Traditional

down in my heart, down in my

heart. I've got that peace that pass - eth un - der - stand - ing

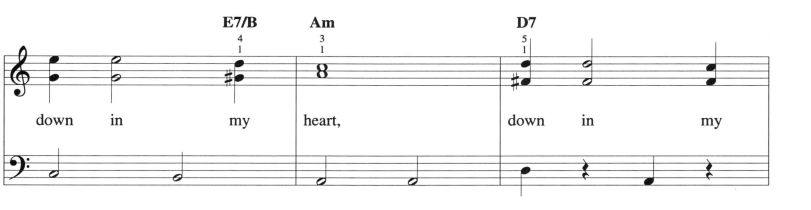

down in my heart, down in my

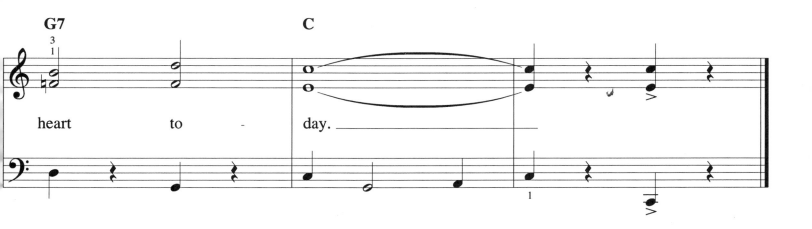

heart to - day. _____

A DREAM IS A WISH YOUR HEART MAKES

from Walt Disney's CINDERELLA

Words and Music by MACK DAVID,
AL HOFFMAN and JERRY LIVINGSTON

faith in your dreams and some - day _____ Your

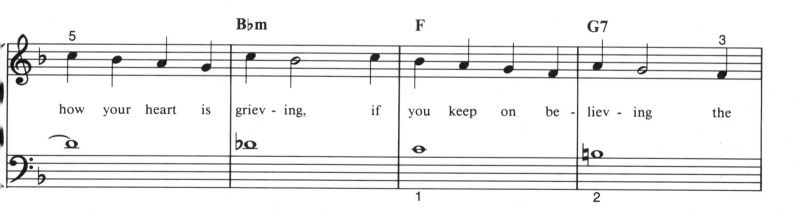

rain - bow will come smil - ing thru, _____ No mat - ter

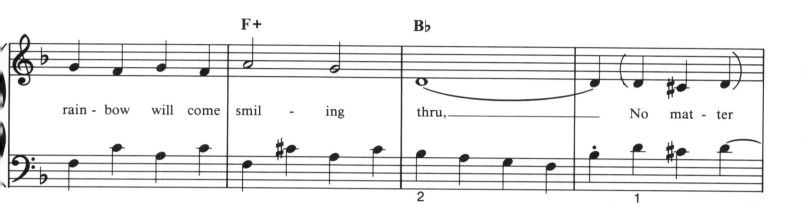

how your heart is griev - ing, if you keep on be - liev - ing the

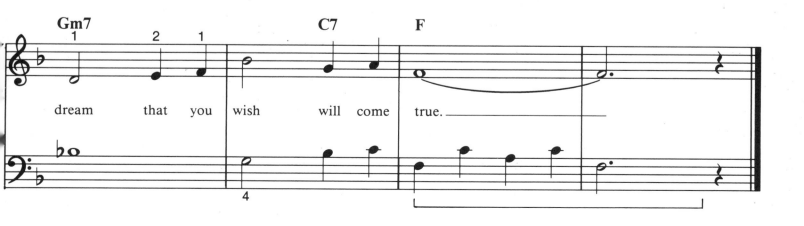

dream that you wish will come true. _____

EENSY WEENSY SPIDER

Traditional

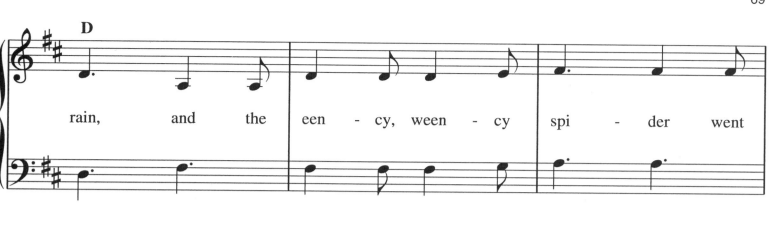

rain, and the een - cy, ween - cy spi - der went

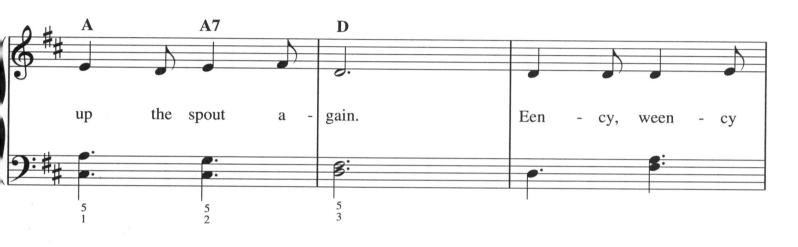

up the spout a - gain. Een - cy, ween - cy

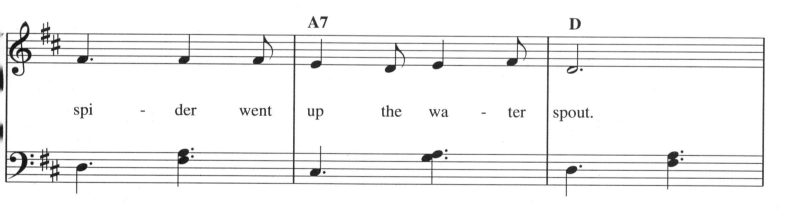

spi - der went up the wa - ter spout.

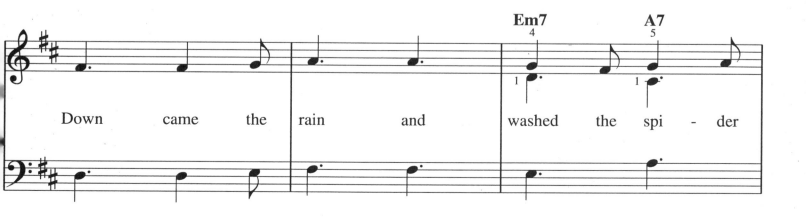

Down came the rain and washed the spi - der

EV'RYBODY WANTS TO BE A CAT

from Walt Disney's THE ARISTOCATS

Words by FLOYD HUDDLESTON
Music by AL RINKER

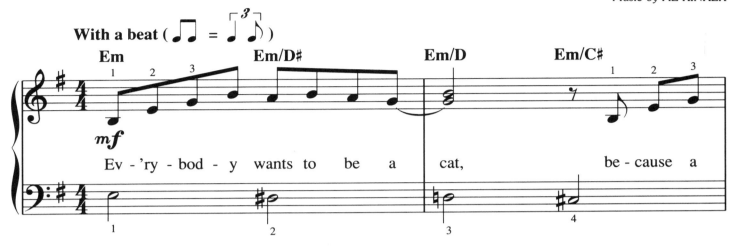

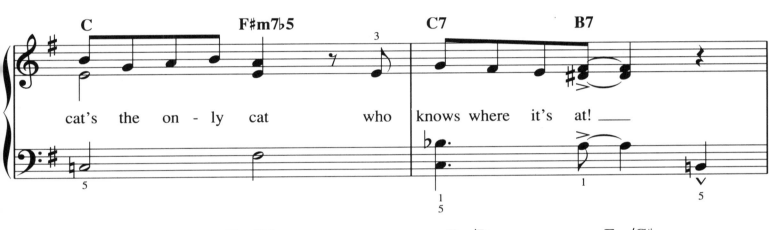

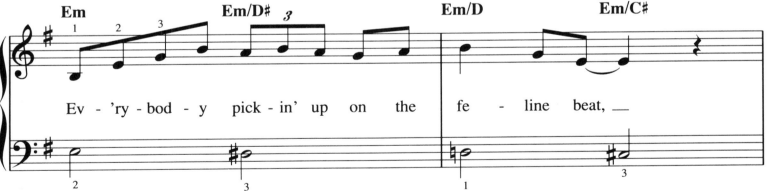

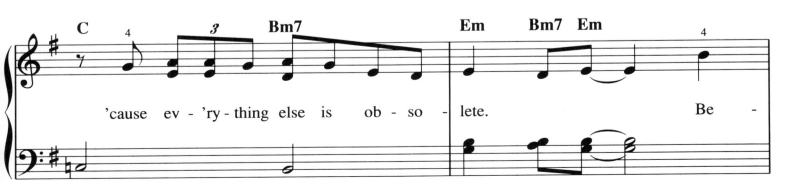

THE FARMER IN THE DELL

Traditional

farm - er takes a wife. Heigh - ho, the

der - ry o! The farm - er takes a wife.

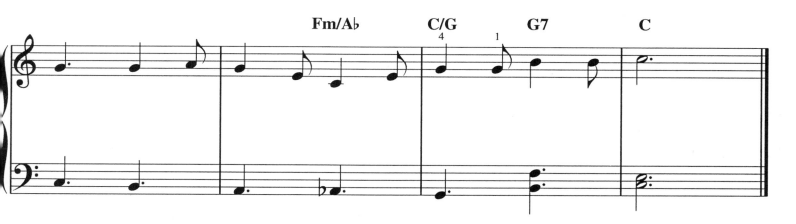

Additional Lyrics

3. The wife takes the child,
   The wife takes the child,
   Heigh-ho, the derry o!
   The wife takes the child.

4. The child takes the nurse,
   The child takes the nurse,
   Heigh-ho, the derry o!
   The child takes the nurse.

5. The nurse takes the dog,
   The nurse takes the dog,
   Heigh-ho, the derry o!
   The nurse takes the dog.

6. The dog takes the cat,
   The dog takes the cat,
   Heigh-ho, the derry o!
   The dog takes the cat.

7. The cat takes the rat,
   The cat takes the rat,
   Heigh-ho, the derry o!
   The cat takes the rat.

8. The rat takes the cheese,
   The rat takes the cheese,
   Heigh-ho, the derry o!
   The rat takes the cheese.

9. The cheese stands alone,
   The cheese stands alone,
   Heigh-ho, the derry o!
   The cheese stands alone.

FRÈRE JACQUES
(Are You Sleeping?)

Traditional

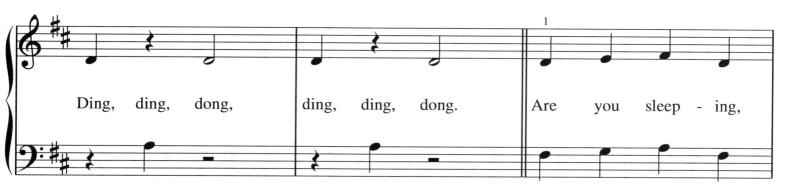

Ding, ding, dong, ding, ding, dong. Are you sleep - ing,

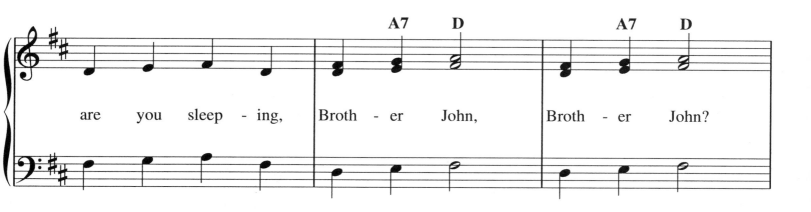

are you sleep - ing, Broth - er John, Broth - er John?

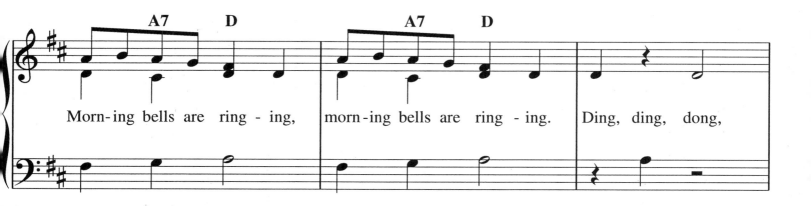

Morn-ing bells are ring - ing, morn-ing bells are ring - ing. Ding, ding, dong,

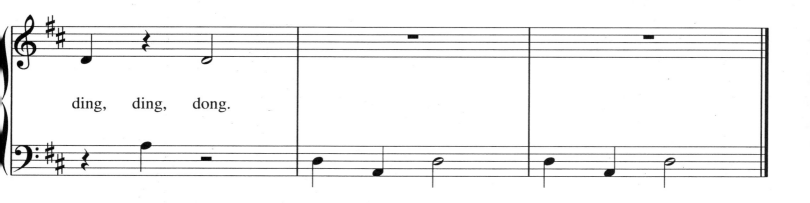

ding, ding, dong.

FRIEND LIKE ME

from Walt Disney's ALADDIN

Lyrics by HOWARD ASHMAN
Music by ALAN MENKEN

Moderately bright

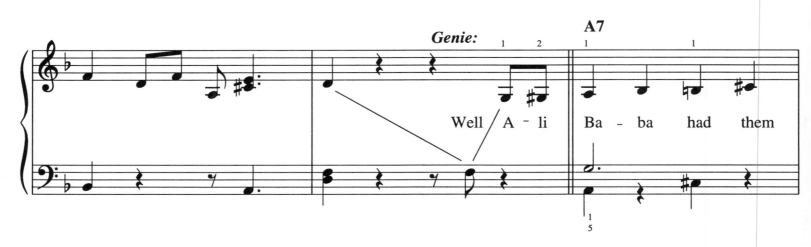

res - tau - rant ___ and I'm your mai - tre d.' C' - mon

whis - per what it is you want. You ain't nev - er had a friend like

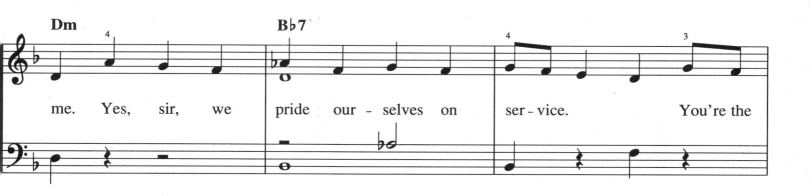

me. Yes, sir, we pride our - selves on ser - vice. You're the

boss, the king, the shah. Say what you wish. ___ It's

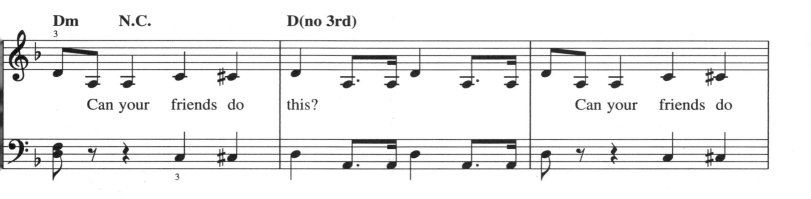

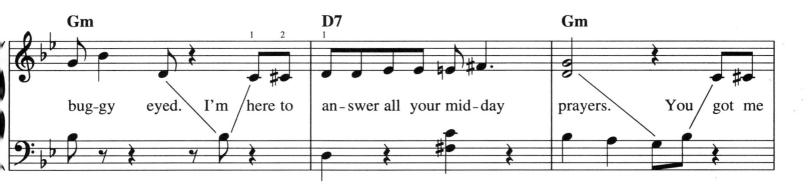

bug-gy eyed. I'm here to an-swer all your mid-day prayers. You got me

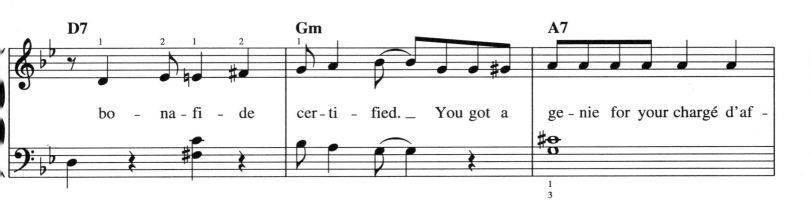

bo — na - fi - de cer-ti - fied. _ You got a ge - nie for your chargé d'af -

faires. I got a pow-er-ful urge to help you out. So what-cha

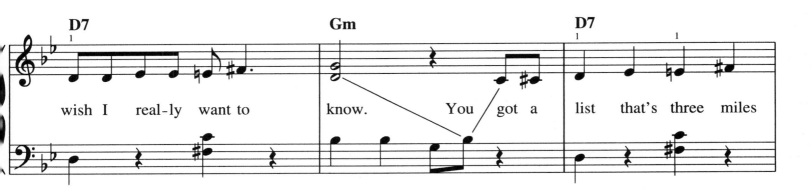

wish I real-ly want to know. You got a list that's three miles

had a   friend. You ain't   nev - er _____   had a _____

friend   like   me.

Wa - ah   ah.

Wa ah   ah.   You ain't nev-er had a friend like   me.   Ha!

add pedal

GETTING TO KNOW YOU
from THE KING AND I

Lyrics by OSCAR HAMMERSTEIN II
Music by RICHARD RODGERS

get - ting to hope you like me.

Get - ting to know you,

put - ting it my way, but nice - ly,

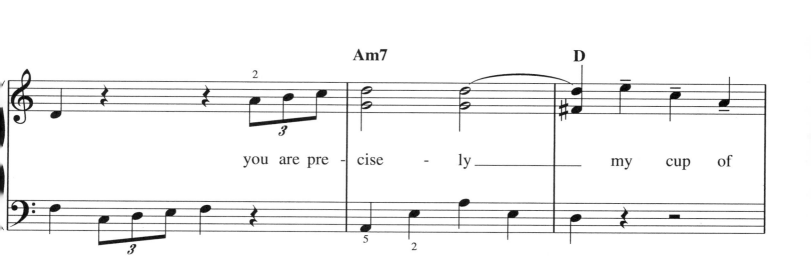

you are pre - cise - ly _____ my cup of

GIVE A LITTLE WHISTLE
from Walt Disney's PINOCCHIO

Words by NED WASHINGTON
Music by LEIGH HARLINE

HAKUNA MATATA

from Walt Disney Pictures' THE LION KING

Music by ELTON JOHN
Lyrics by TIM RICE

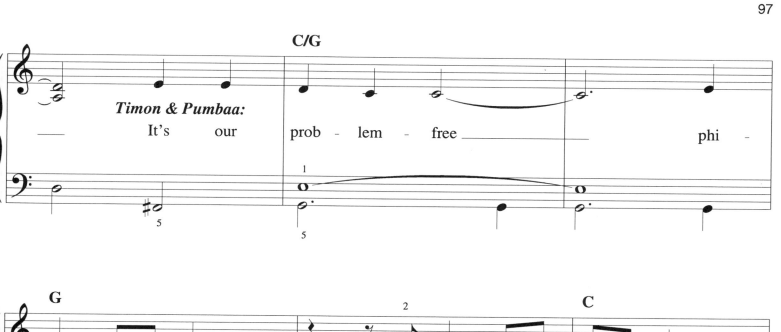

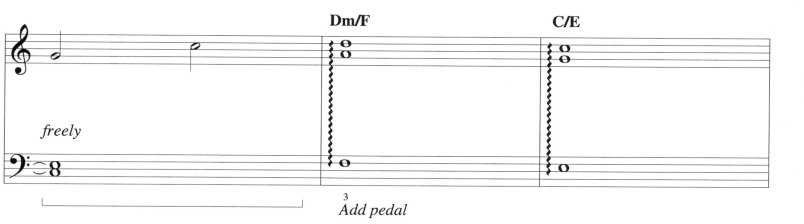

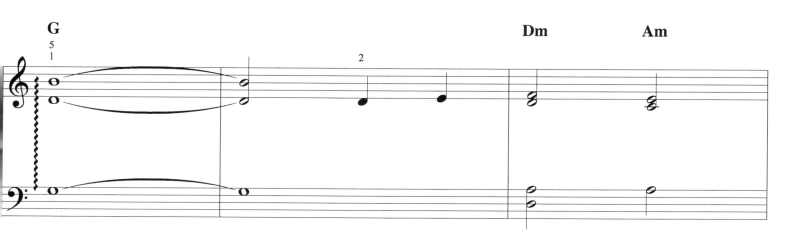

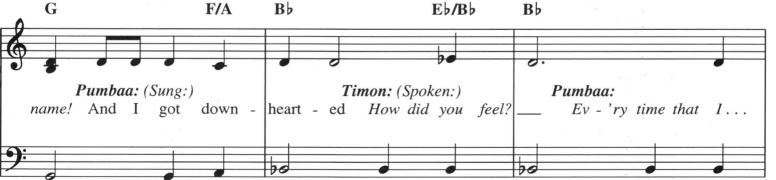

Timon:
Hey, Pumbaa, not in front of the kids. *Pumbaa:* Oh, sorry.

Timon & Pumbaa:
Ha - ku - na ma -

ta - ta... what a won - der - ful phrase.

Ha - ku - na ma - ta - ta ain't no pass - ing

craze.   ***Simba:*** It means no wor - ries

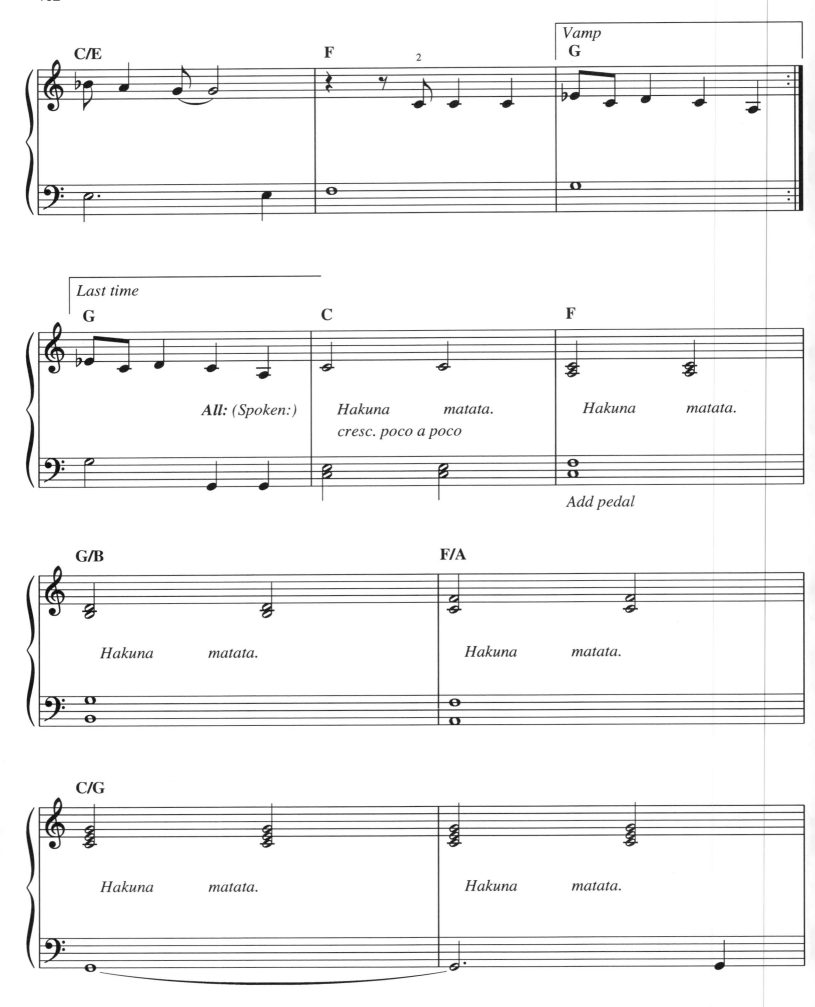

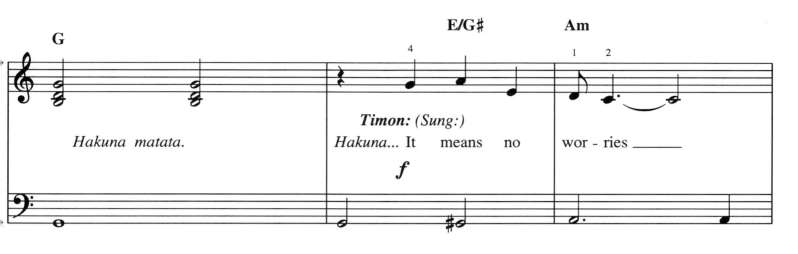

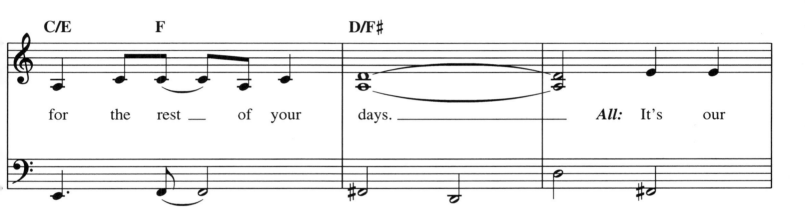

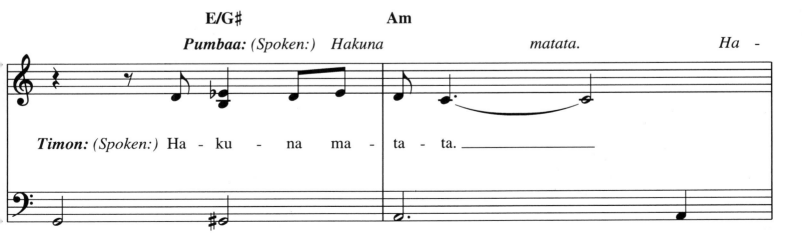

HAPPY TRAILS
from the Television Series THE ROY ROGERS SHOW

Words and Music by
DALE EVANS

HEIGH-HO

The Dwarf's Marching Song from Walt Disney's SNOW WHITE AND THE SEVEN DWARFS

Words by LARRY MOREY
Music by FRANK CHURCHILL

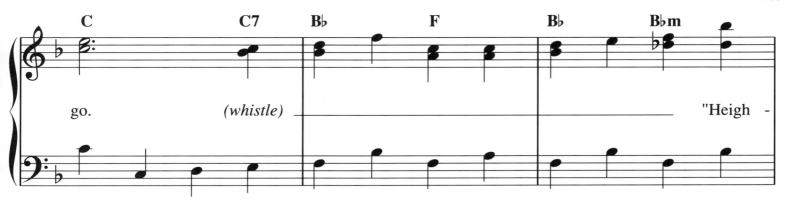

go.　　　　　(whistle) _____　　　"Heigh -

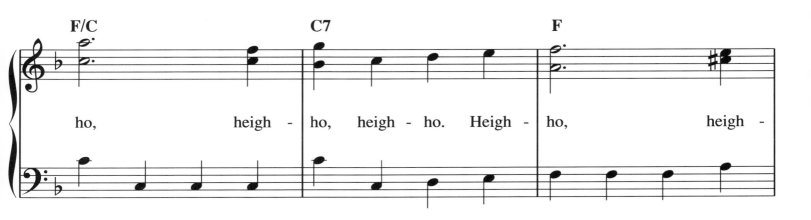

ho,　　heigh - ho, heigh - ho. Heigh - ho,　　heigh -

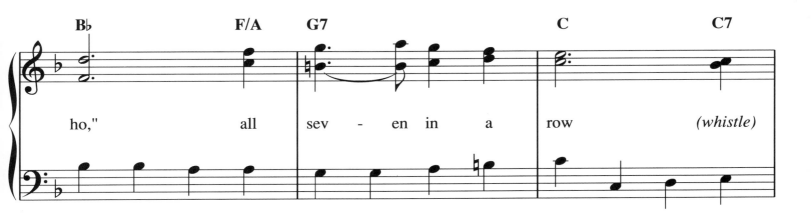

ho,"　　all　sev - en　in　a　row　　(whistle)

_____　with a "Heigh,　heigh - ho."

HAPPY, HAPPY BIRTHDAY TO YOU

from Walt Disney Records' SPLASHDANCE Album

Words and Music by MICHAEL SILVERSHER
and PATRICIA SILVERSHER

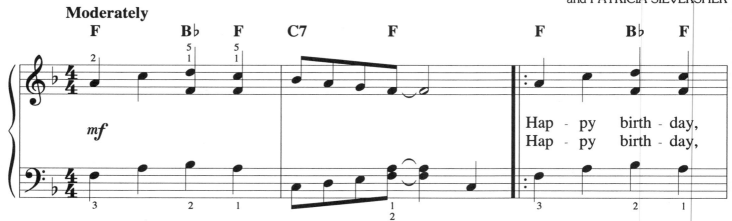
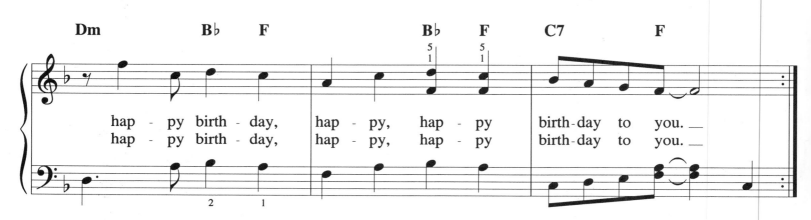

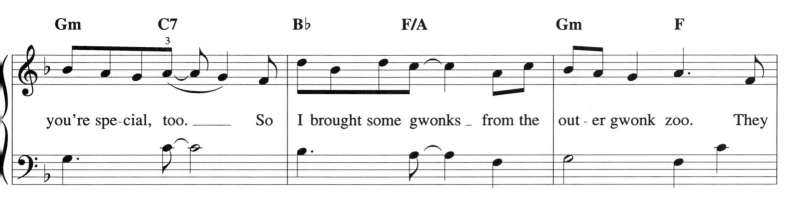

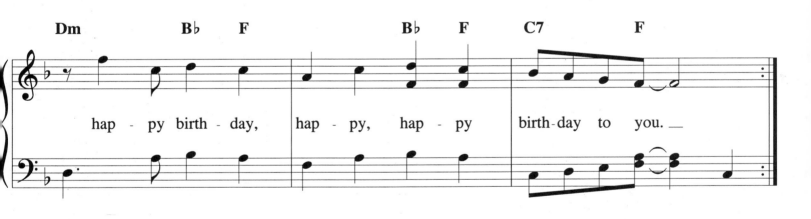

once - a - year oc - ca - sion. __ A par - ty ____ is

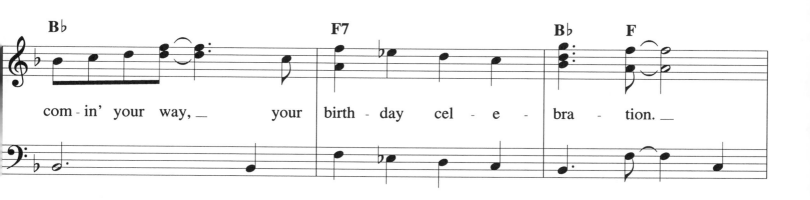

com - in' your way, __ your birth - day cel - e - bra - tion. __

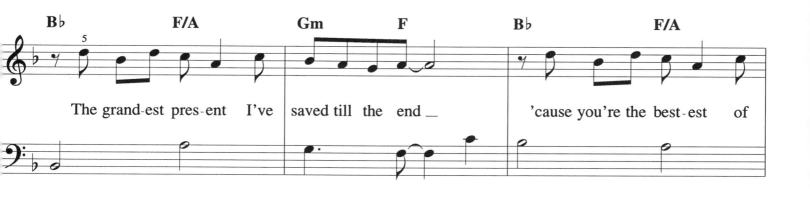

The grand-est pres-ent I've saved till the end __ 'cause you're the best-est of

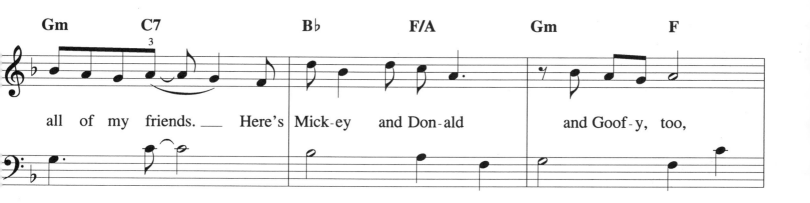

all of my friends. __ Here's Mick-ey and Don-ald and Goof-y, too,

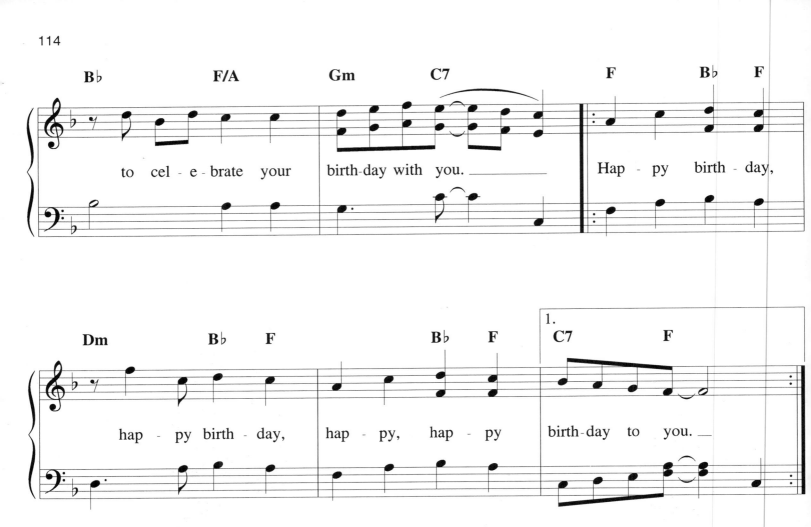

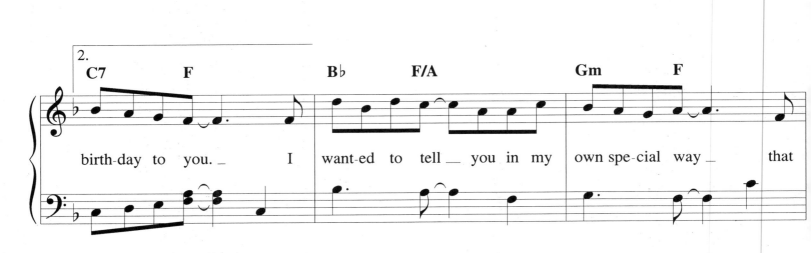

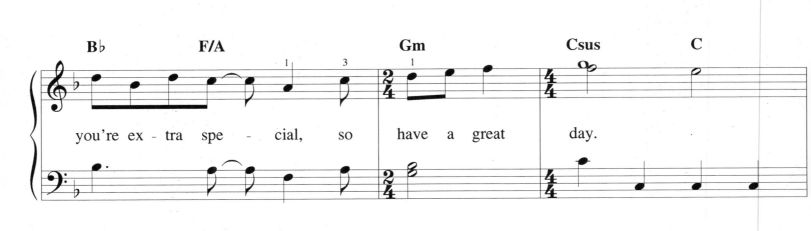

HELLO MUDDUH, HELLO FADDUH!
(A Letter from Camp)

Words by ALLAN SHERMAN
Music by LOU BUSCH

hik - ing with Joe Spi - vy, He de - vel - oped poi - son
don't want this should scare ya, But my bunk mate has ma -

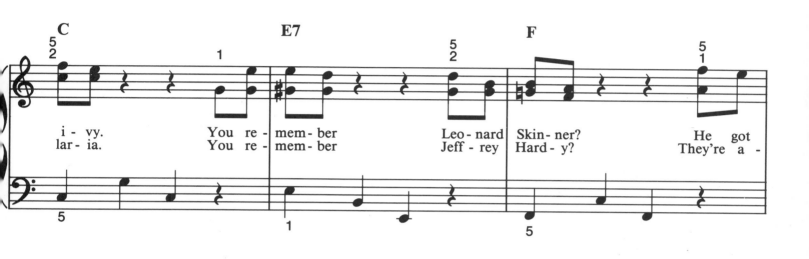

i - vy. You re - mem - ber Leo - nard Skin - ner? He got
lar - ia. You re - mem - ber Jeff - rey Hard - y? They're a -

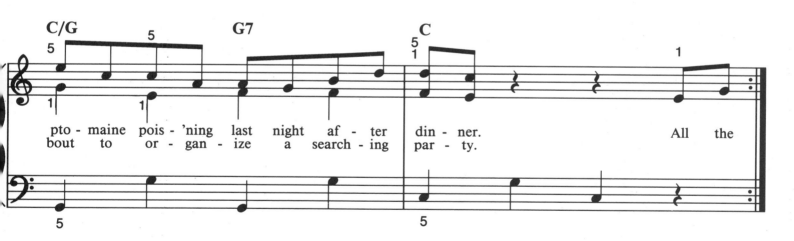

pto - maine pois - 'ning last night af - ter din - ner. All the
bout to or - gan - ize a search - ing par - ty.

Take me home, oh Mud - duh, Fad - duh, take me
Take me home, I prom - ise I will not make

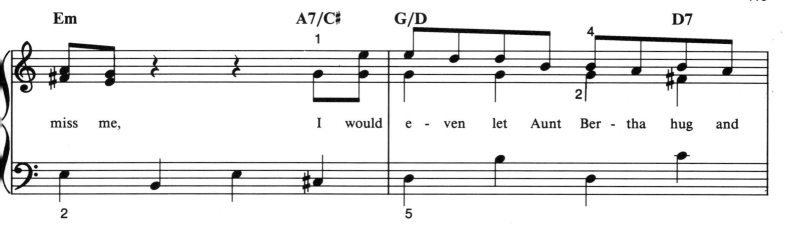

miss me,   I would e - ven let Aunt Ber - tha hug and

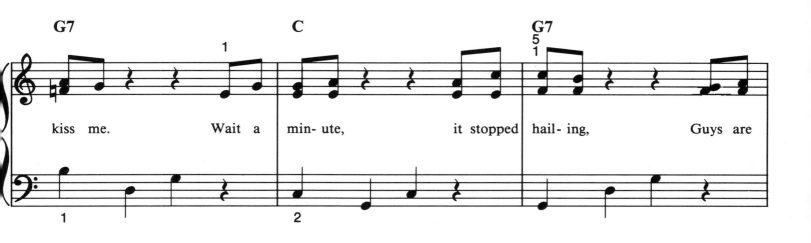

kiss me.   Wait a min- ute,   it stopped hail- ing,   Guys are

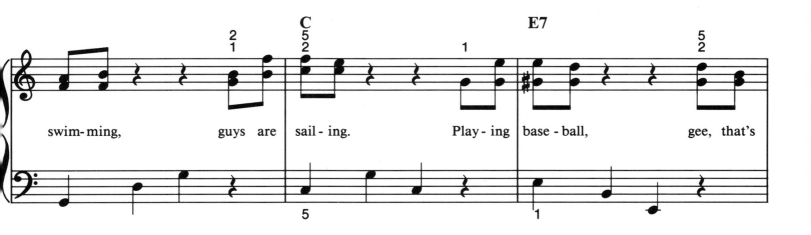

swim-ming,   guys are sail - ing.   Play - ing base - ball,   gee, that's

bet - ter.   Mud-duh, Fad-duh, kind- ly dis - re - gard this let - ter!   *sfz*

HEY DIDDLE DIDDLE

Traditional

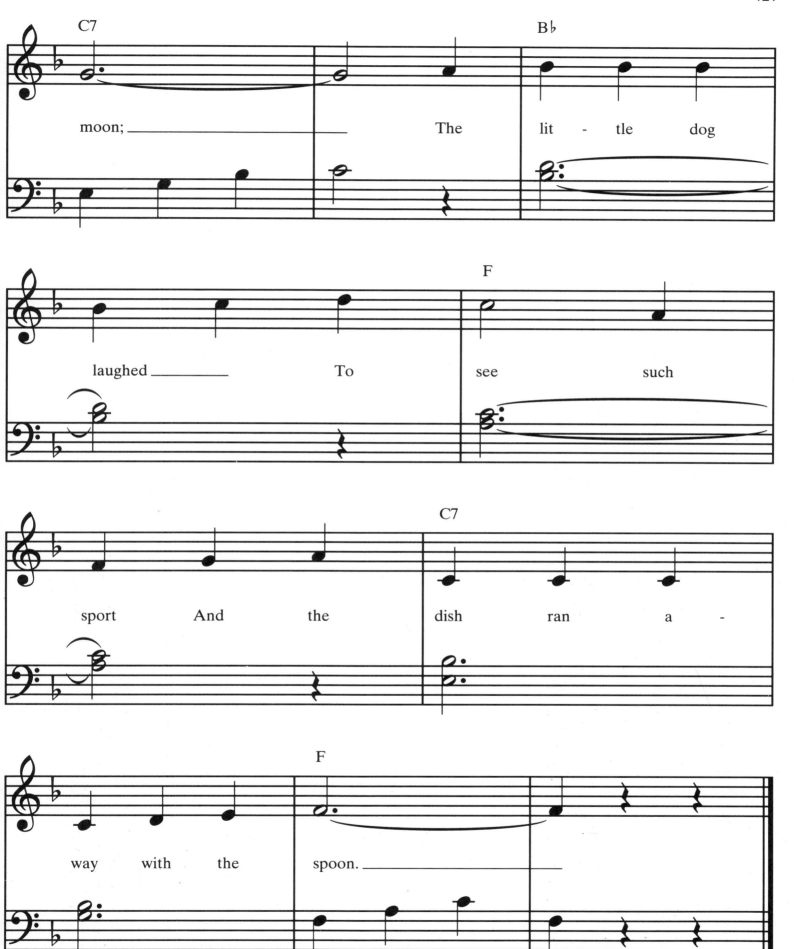

HICKORY DICKORY DOCK

Traditional

Lyrics:

Hick - or - y, dick - or - y, dock. The mouse ran up the clock. The clock struck one; the mouse ran down, hick - or - y, dick - or - y, dock.

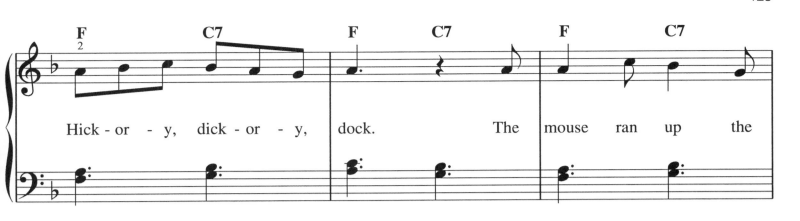

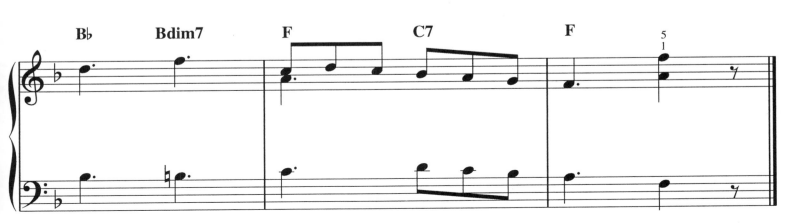

HOW MUCH IS THAT DOGGIE IN THE WINDOW

Words and Music by
BOB MERRILL

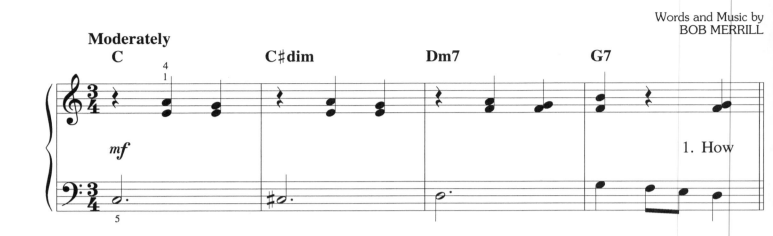

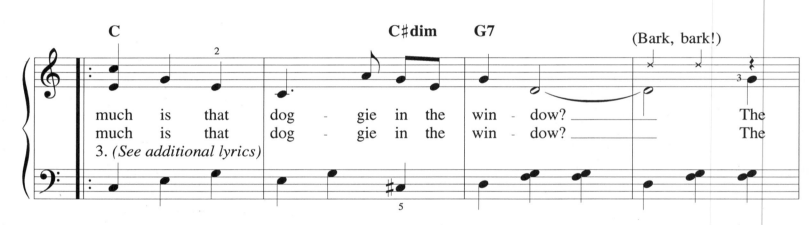

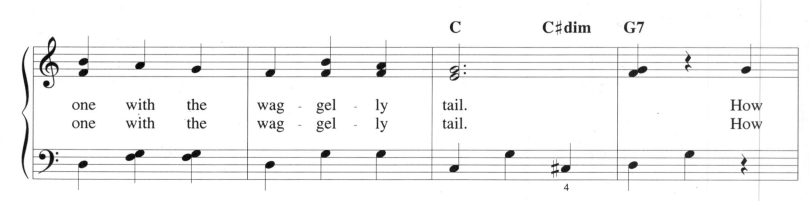

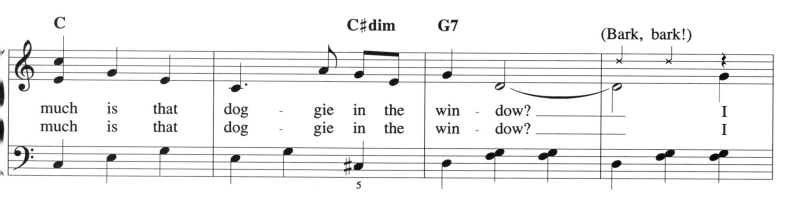

much   is   that   dog - gie   in   the   win - dow? _____   I
much   is   that   dog - gie   in   the   win - dow? _____   I

(Bark, bark!)

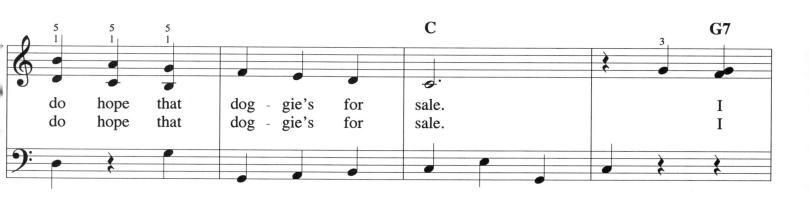

do   hope   that   dog - gie's   for   sale. _____   I
do   hope   that   dog - gie's   for   sale. _____   I

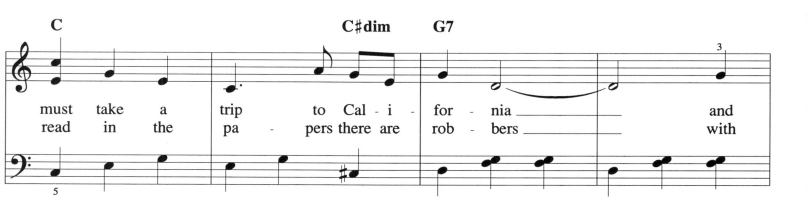

must   take   a   trip   to   Cal - i - for - nia _____   and
read   in   the   pa - pers   there   are   rob - bers _____   with

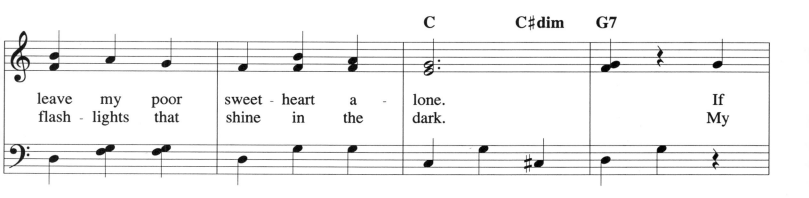

leave   my   poor   sweet - heart   a - lone. _____   If
flash - lights   that   shine   in   the   dark. _____   My

Additional Lyrics

3. I don't want a bunny or a kitty.
   I don't want a parrot that talks,
   I don't want a bowl of little fishies;
   He can't take a goldfish for walks.
   How much is that doggie in the window?
   The one with the waggely tail.
   How much is that doggie in the window?
   I do hope that doggie's for sale.

I DON'T WANT TO LIVE ON THE MOON

from the Television Series SESAME STREET

Words and Music by
JEFF MOSS

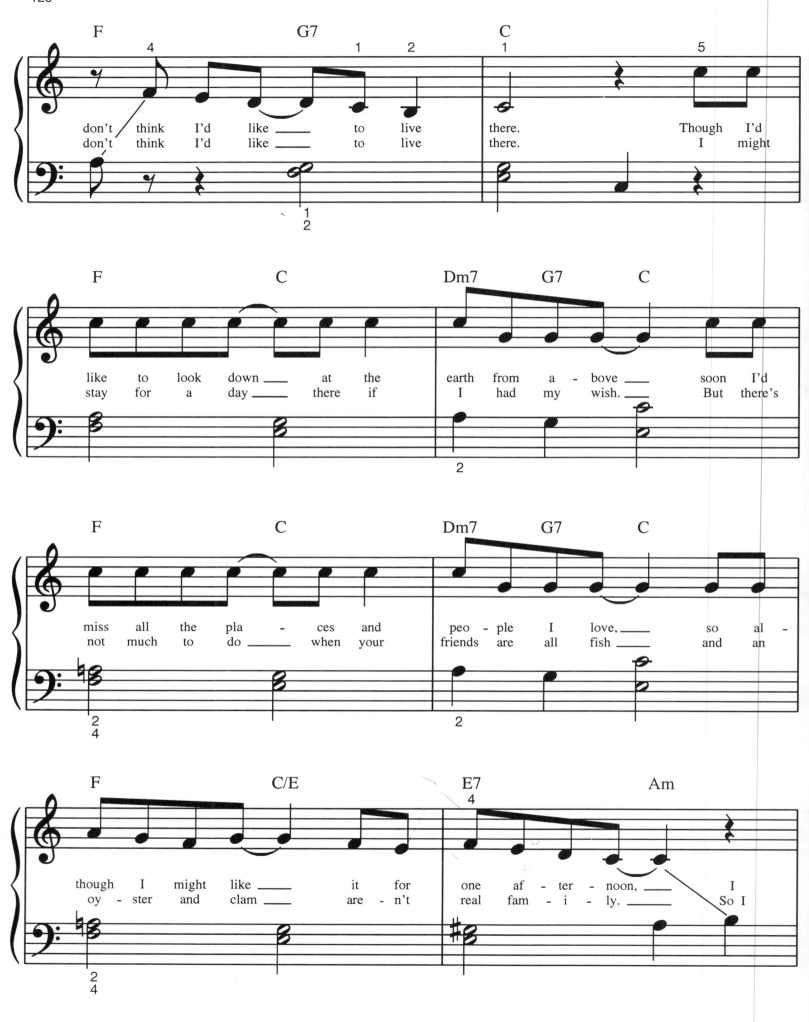

129

I WHISTLE A HAPPY TUNE

from THE KING AND I

Lyrics by OSCAR HAMMERSTEIN II
Music by RICHARD RODGERS

knows I'm a - fraid._____ The re -

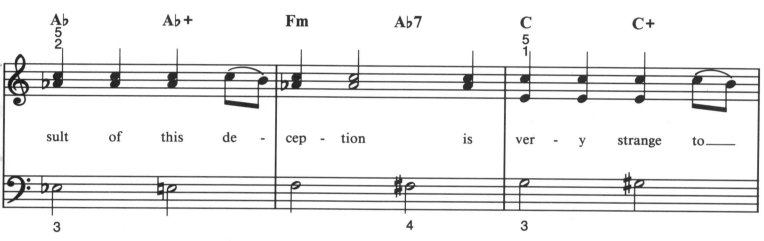

sult of this de - cep - tion is ver - y strange to___

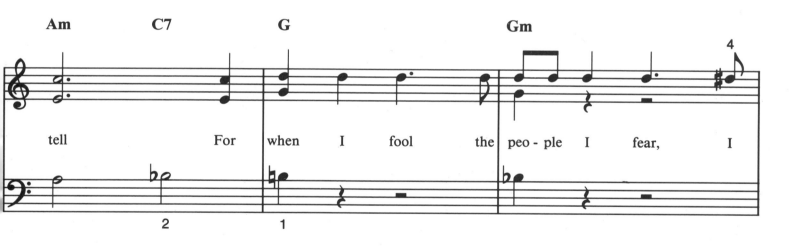

tell For when I fool the peo - ple I fear, I

fool my - self as well! I whis - tle a hap - py

tune   And ev-'ry sin-gle time   The hap-pi-ness in the

tune   con-vin-ces me that I'm   not a-fraid.

Make be-lieve you're brave   And the

trick will take you far.   You may be as

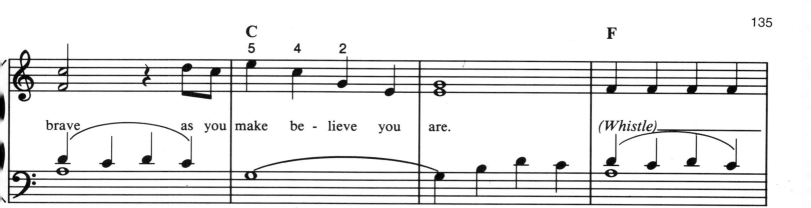

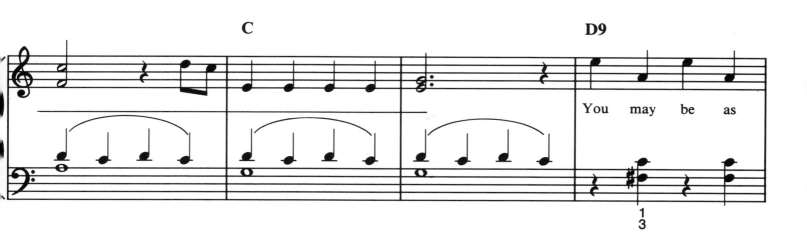

I'M LATE
from Walt Disney's ALICE IN WONDERLAND

Words by BOB HILLIARD
Music by SAMMY FAIN

Cm

when I wave, I lose the time I

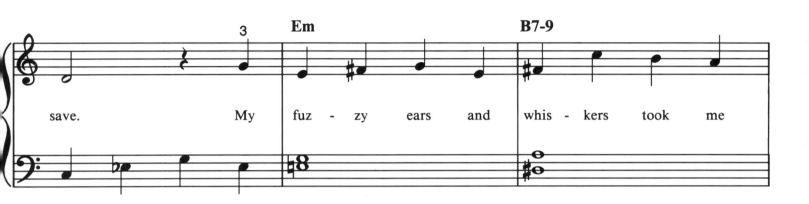

Em   **B7-9**

save. My fuz - zy ears and whis - kers took me

Em   **Am6**   **Em**   **G7**

too much time to shave. I run and then I

C6   **G7**   **C6**

hop, hop, hop, I wish that I could fly. There's

I'M POPEYE THE SAILOR MAN

Theme from the Paramount Cartoon POPEYE THE SAILOR

Words and Music by
SAMMY LERNER

140

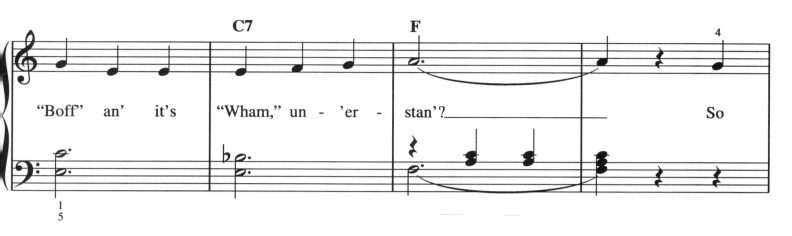

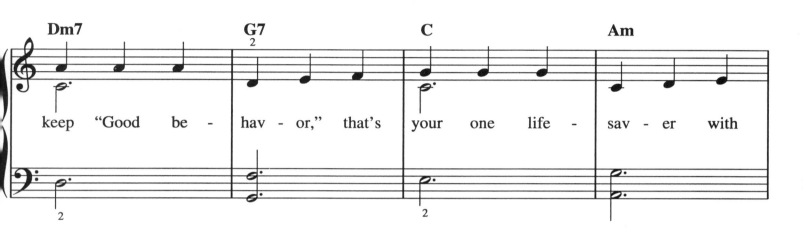

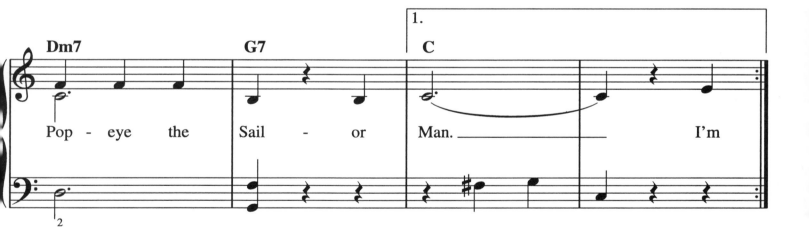

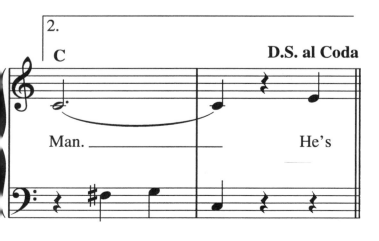

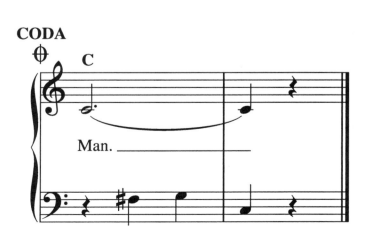

I'VE BEEN WORKING ON THE RAILROAD

American Folksong

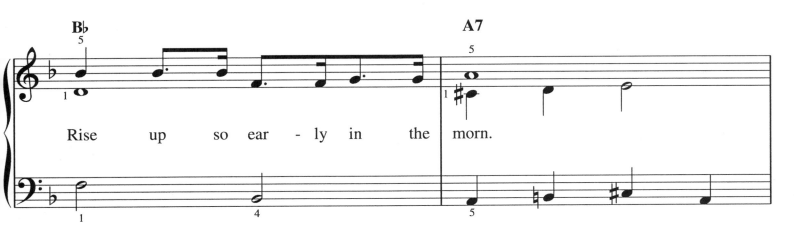

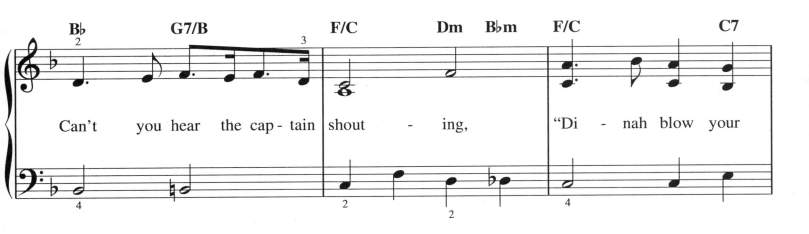

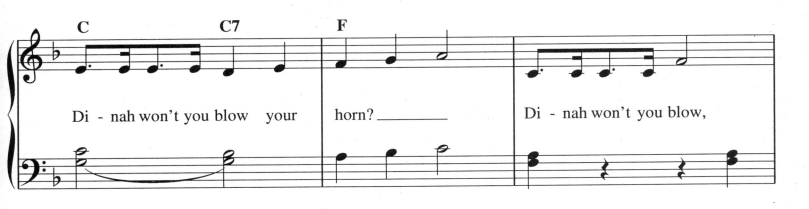

144

"Fee, fi, fid - dle - ee - i - o, fee, fi, fid - dle - ee - i -

o. _____ Fee, fi, fid - dle - ee - i - o."

strum - min' on the old ban - jo.

IN MY OWN LITTLE CORNER

from CINDERELLA

Lyrics by OSCAR HAMMERSTEIN II
Music by RICHARD RODGERS

JOHN JACOB JINGLEHEIMER SCHMIDT

Traditional

IT'S A SMALL WORLD
from Disneyland and Walt Disney World's IT'S A SMALL WORLD

Words and Music by RICHARD M. SHERMAN
and ROBERT B. SHERMAN

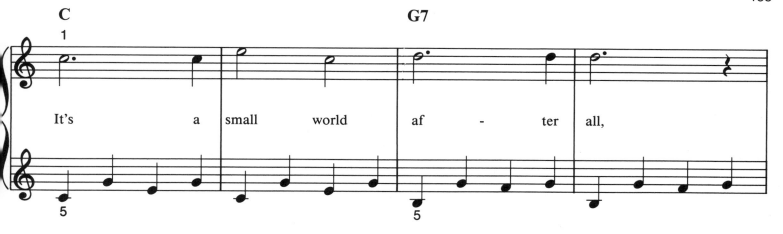

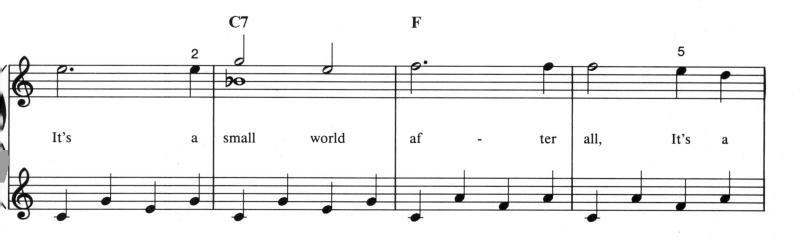

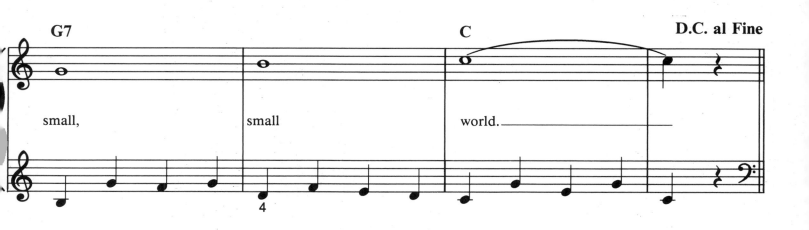

JACK AND JILL

Traditional

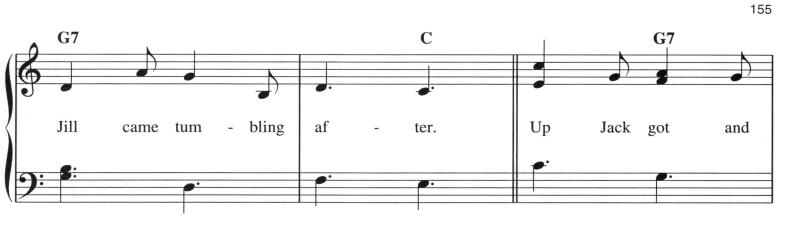

Jill came tum - bling af - ter. Up Jack got and

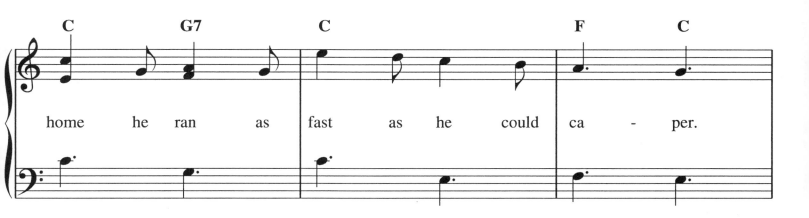

home he ran as fast as he could ca - per.

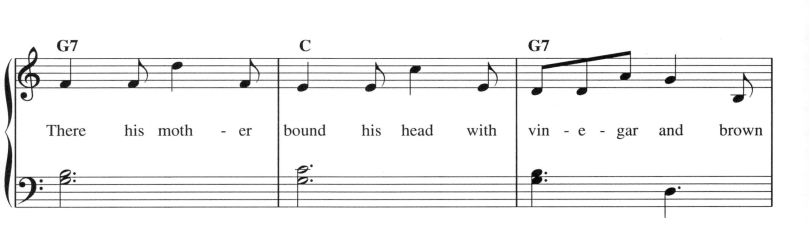

There his moth - er bound his head with vin - e - gar and brown

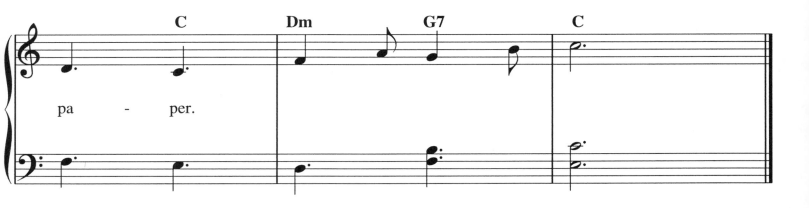

pa - per.

JESUS LOVES ME

Words by ANNA WARNER
Music by WILLIAM BRADBURY

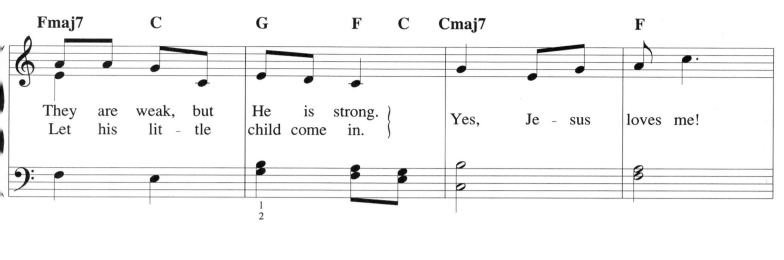

They are weak, but He is strong.
Let his lit - tle child come in. } Yes, Je - sus loves me!

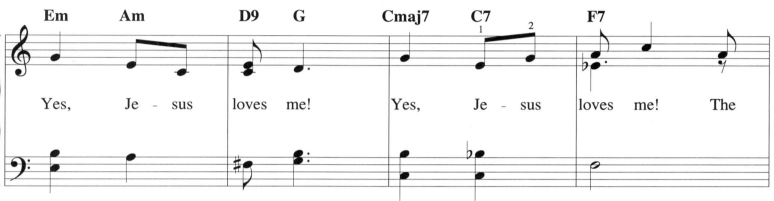

Yes, Je - sus loves me! Yes, Je - sus loves me! The

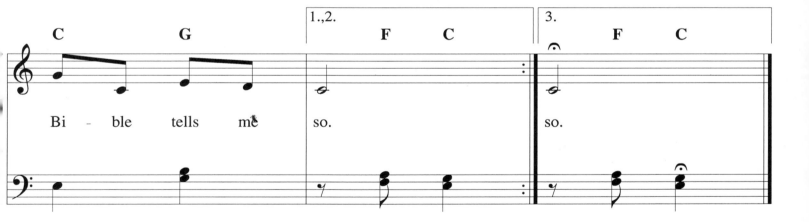

Bi - ble tells me so. so.

Additional Lyrics

3. Jesus, take this heart of mine,
   Make it pure and wholly Thine,
   Thou hast bled and died for me;
   I will henceforth live for Thee.
   Yes, Jesus loves me!
   Yes, Jesus loves me!
   Yes, Jesus loves me!
   The Bible tells me so.

JESUS LOVES THE LITTLE CHILDREN

Traditional

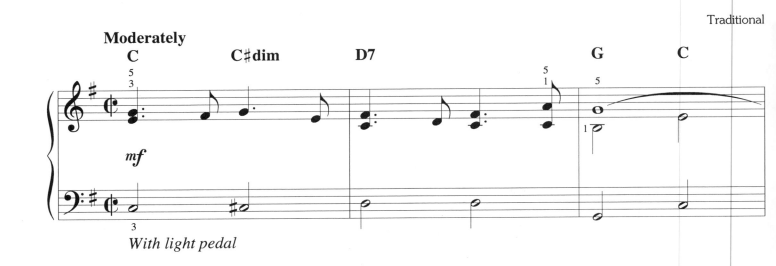

With light pedal

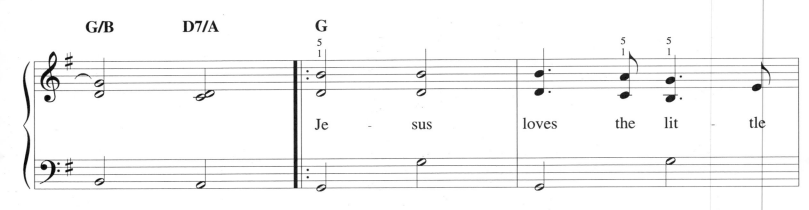

Je - sus loves the lit - tle

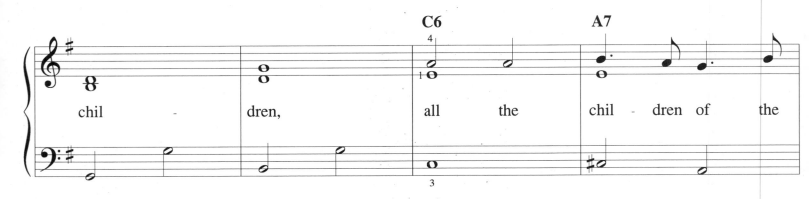

chil - dren, all the chil - dren of the

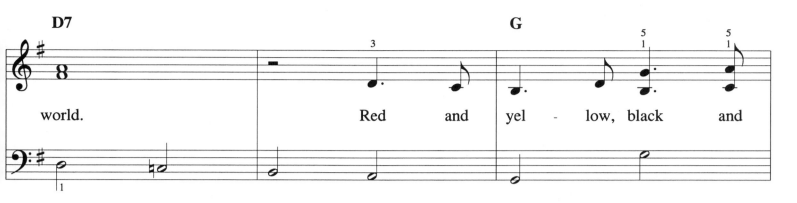

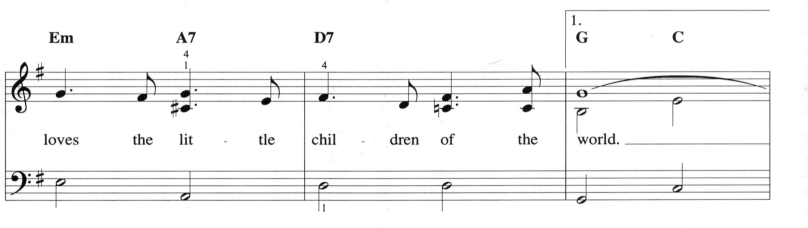

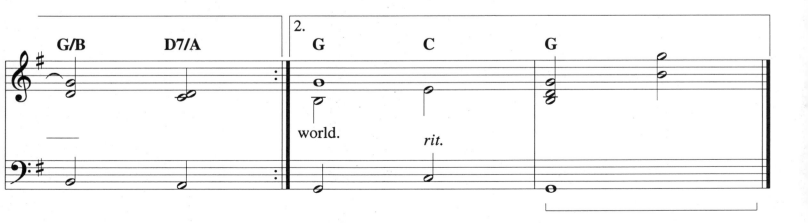

LAVENDER BLUE
(Dilly Dilly)
from Walt Disney's SO DEAR TO MY HEART

Words by LARRY MOREY
Music by ELIOT DANIEL

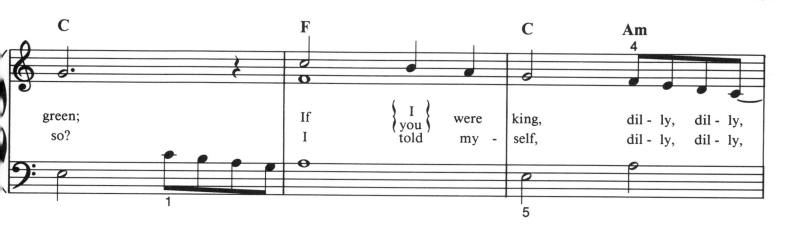

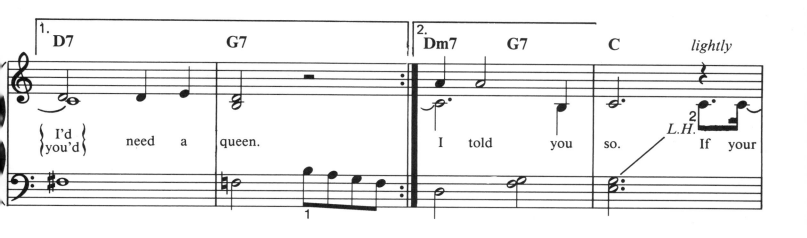

LITTLE APRIL SHOWER
from Walt Disney's BAMBI

Words by LARRY MOREY
Music by FRANK CHURCHILL

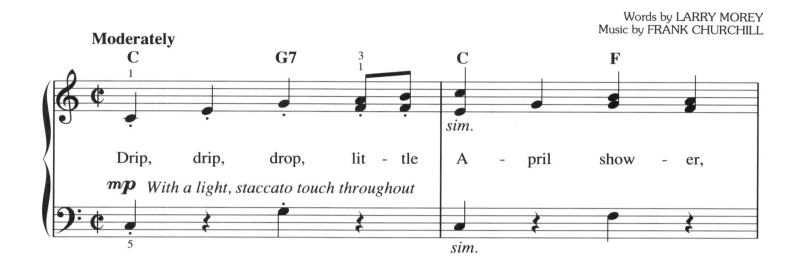

Drip, drip, drop, lit-tle A-pril show-er,

With a light, staccato touch throughout

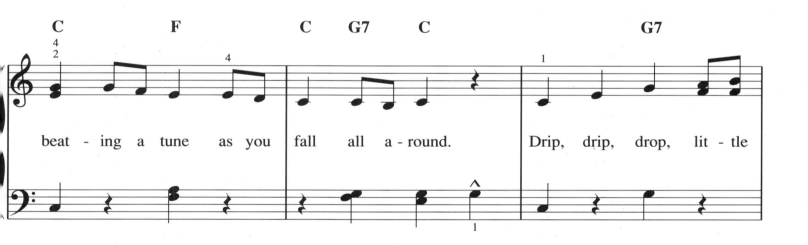

beat-ing a tune as you fall all a-round. Drip, drip, drop, lit-tle

A-pril show-er, what can com-pare with your beau-ti-ful sound.

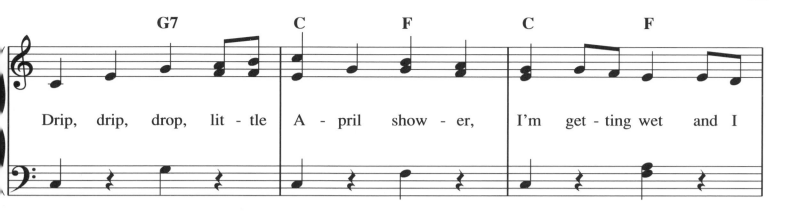

Drip, drip, drop, lit - tle | A - pril show - er, | I'm get - ting wet and I

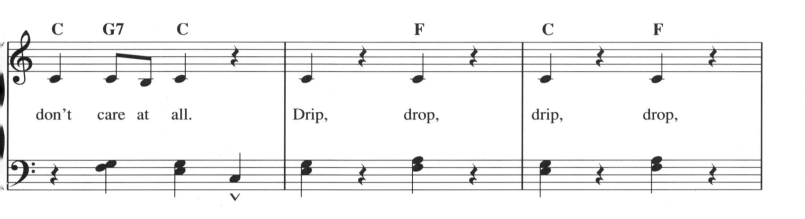

don't care at all. | Drip, drop, | drip, drop,

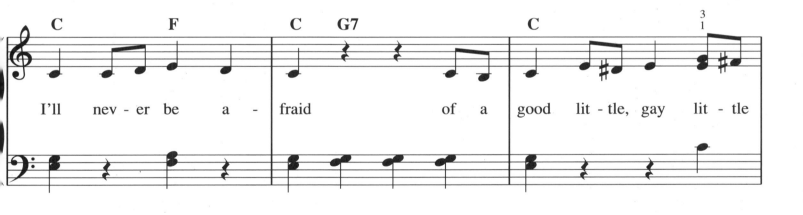

I'll nev - er be a - | fraid | of a | good lit - tle, gay lit - tle

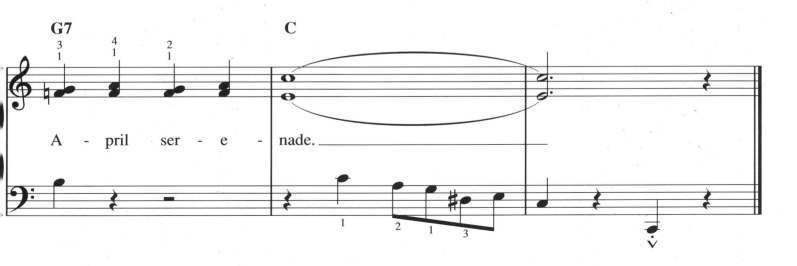

A - pril ser - e - nade. _____

LET ME ENTERTAIN YOU

from GYPSY

Words by STEPHEN SONDHEIM
Music by JULE STYNE

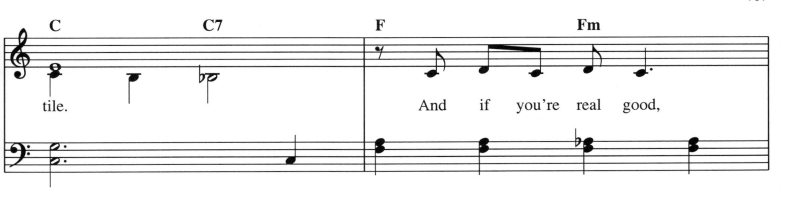

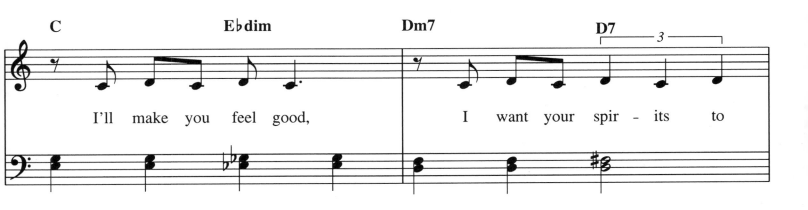

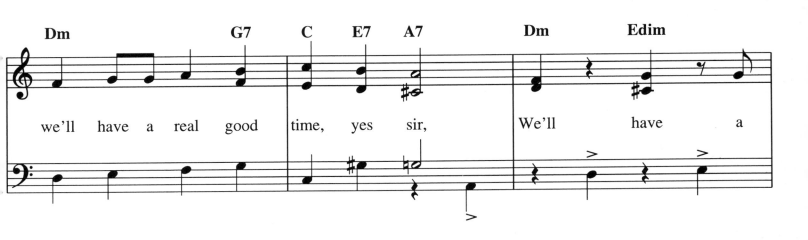

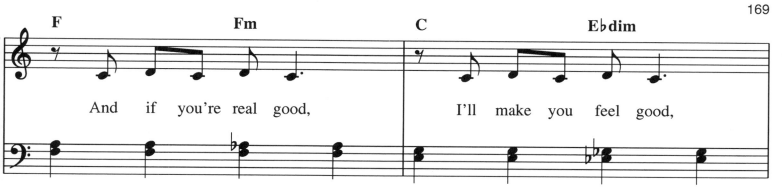

And if you're real good, I'll make you feel good,

I want your spir - its to climb. Just let me en - ter -

tain you, And we'll have a real good time, yes sir,

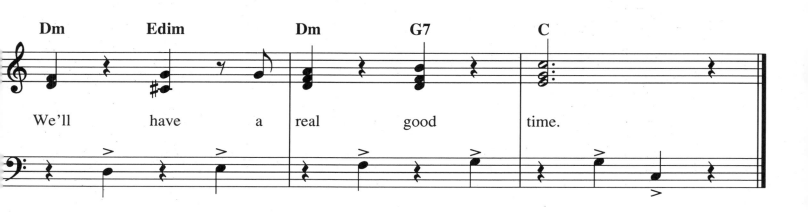

We'll have a real good time.

LITTLE BO-PEEP

Traditional

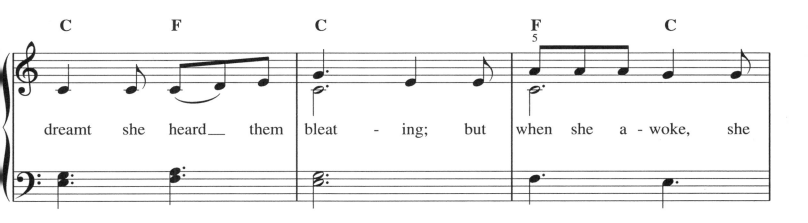

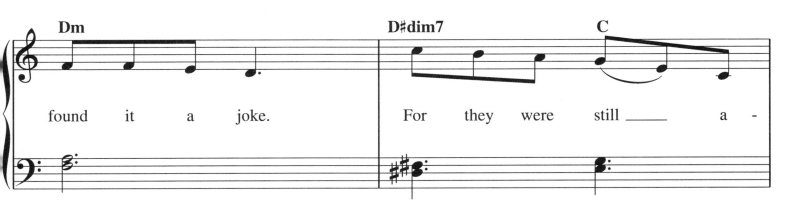

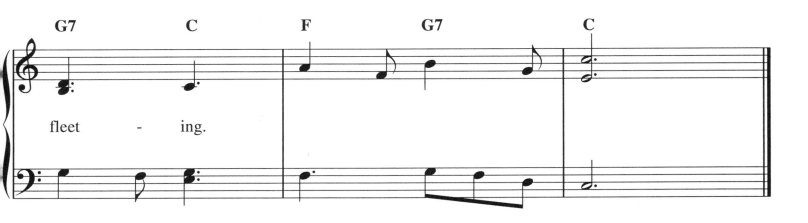

LITTLE PEOPLE
from LES MISÉRABLES

Music by CLAUDE-MICHEL SCHÖNBERG
Original Text by ALAIN BOUBLIL and JEAN-MARC NATEL
Lyrics by HERBERT KRETZMER

worm can roll a stone,__ a bee can sting a bear,__ a fly can fly a-round Ver-sailles 'cos

To Coda

flies don't care! _ A spar-row in a hat can make a hap-py home, a

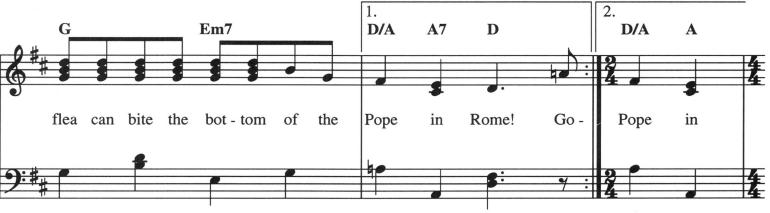

flea can bite the bot-tom of the Pope in Rome! Go- Pope in

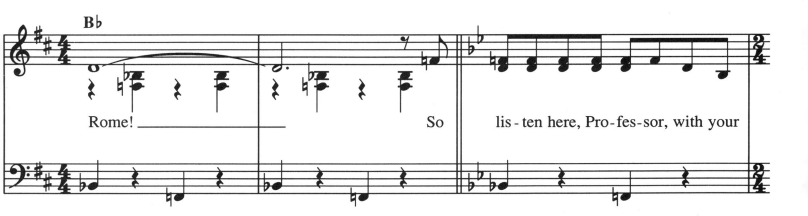

Rome! _____ So lis-ten here, Pro-fes-sor, with your

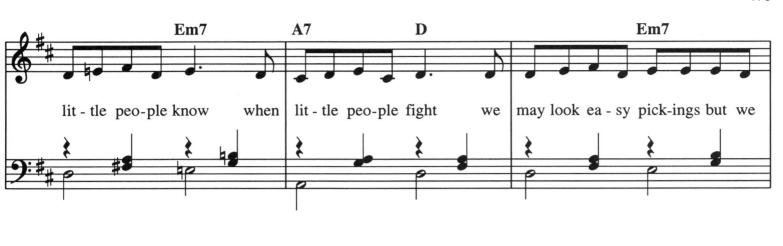

lit - tle peo-ple know when lit - tle peo-ple fight we may look ea - sy pick-ings but we

got some bite! So nev-er kick a dog be-cause it's just a pup. You bet-ter run for cov-er when the

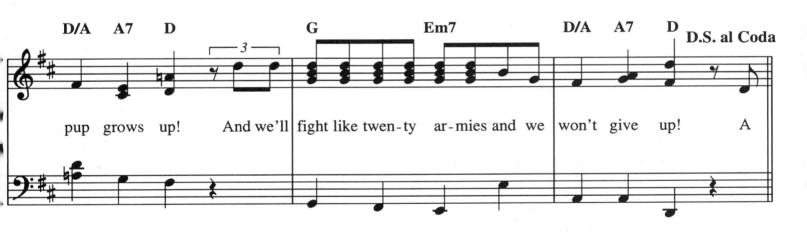

pup grows up! And we'll fight like twen-ty ar-mies and we won't give up! A

CODA

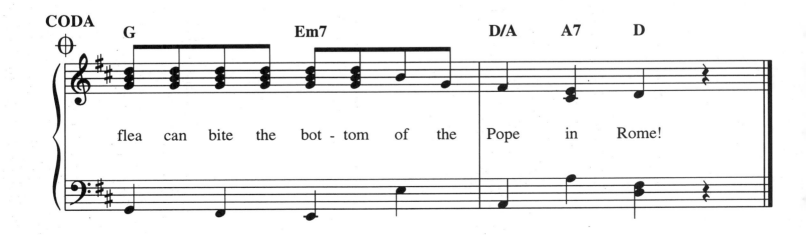

flea can bite the bot-tom of the Pope in Rome!

LONDON BRIDGE

Traditional

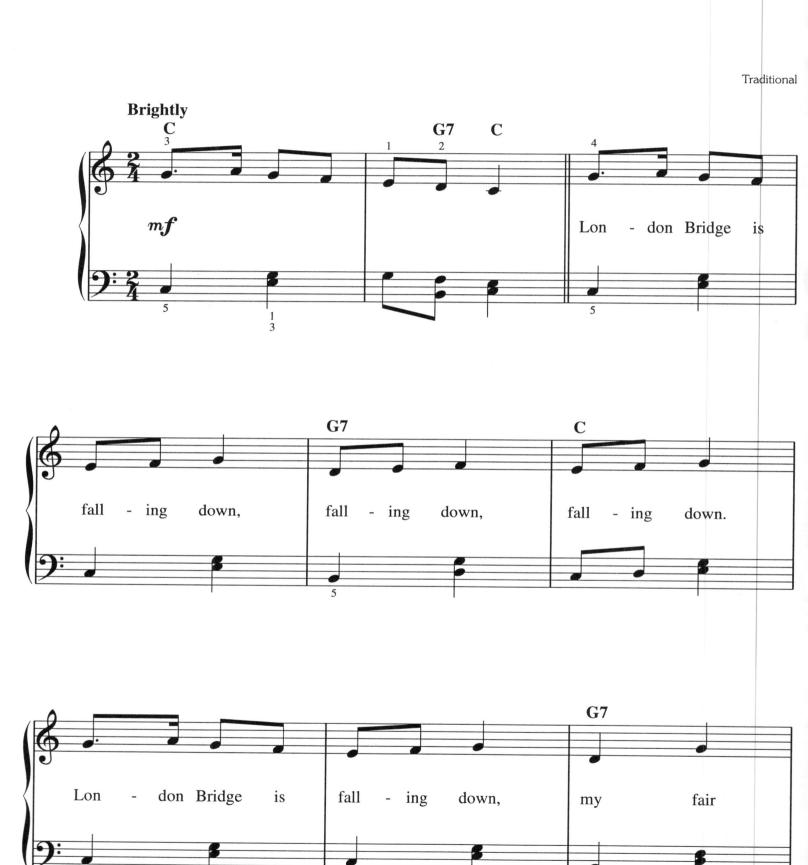

THE LORD IS GOOD TO ME
from Walt Disney's MELODY TIME

Words and Music by KIM GANNON
and WALTER KENT

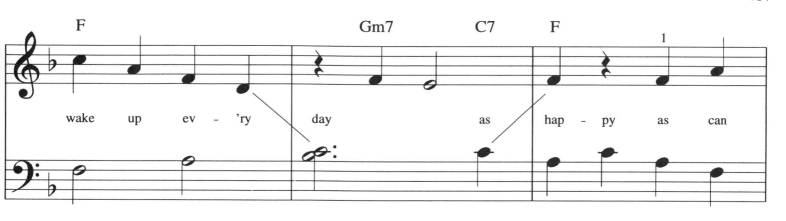

MARY HAD A LITTLE LAMB

Words by SARAH JOSEPHA HALE
Traditional Music

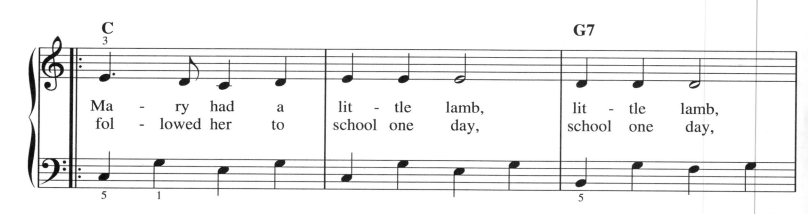

fleece was white as snow.
was a - gainst as the rules. It

Ev - 'ry - where that
made the child - ren

Ma - ry went,
laugh and play,

Ma - ry went,
laugh and play,

Ma - ry went.
laugh and play. It

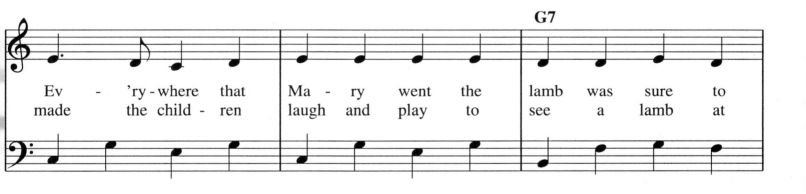

Ev - 'ry - where that
made the child - ren

Ma - ry went the
laugh and play to

lamb was sure to
see a lamb at

1.
C

go. It

2.
school.

MICHAEL ROW THE BOAT ASHORE

Traditional Folksong

MICKEY MOUSE MARCH

from Walt Disney's THE MICKEY MOUSE CLUB

Words and Music by
JIMMIE DODD

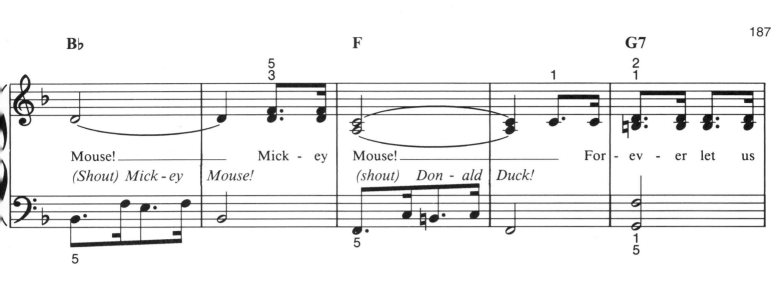

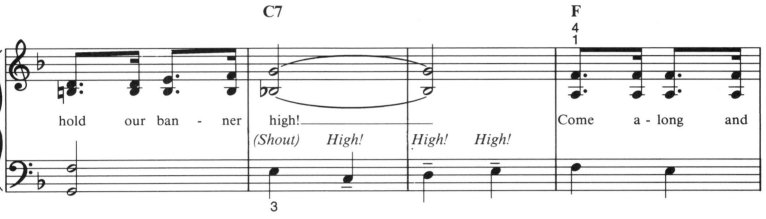

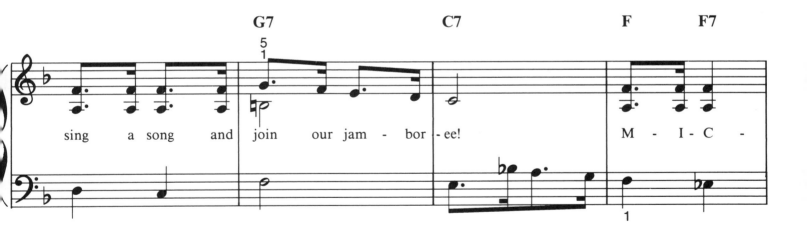

THE MUFFIN MAN

Traditional

muf - fin man who   lives   in   Dru - ry

Lane?   Oh,   yes,   we   know   the   muf - fin man,   the

muf - fin man,   the   muf - fin man.   Oh,   yes,   we   know   the

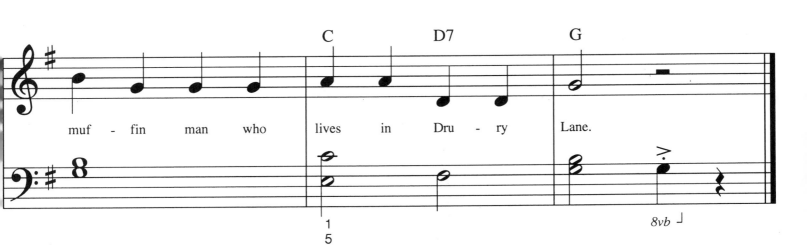

muf - fin man who   lives   in   Dru - ry   Lane.

THE MULBERRY BUSH

Traditional

Here   we   go   'round   the   mul - ber - ry   bush,   so
This   is   the   way   we   wash   our   clothes,   so

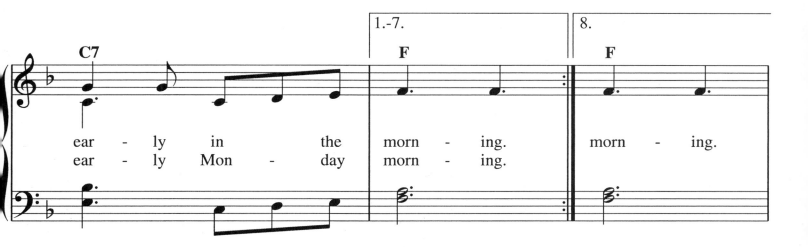

ear - ly   in   the   morn - ing.   morn - ing.
ear - ly   Mon - day   morn - ing.

Additional Lyrics

3. This is the way we iron our clothes, etc.
   So early Tuesday morning.

4. This is the way we scrub the floor, etc.
   So early Wednesday morning.

5. This is the way we mend our clothes, etc.
   So early Thursday morning.

6. This is the way we sweep the house, etc.
   So early Friday morning.

7. This is the way we bake our bread, etc.
   So early Saturday morning.

8. This is the way we go to church, etc.
   So early Sunday morning.

MY BONNIE LIES OVER THE OCEAN

Flowing and spirited

Traditional

MY FAVORITE THINGS
from THE SOUND OF MUSIC

Lyrics by OSCAR HAMMERSTEIN II
Music by RICHARD RODGERS

These are a few of my fa - vor - ite things.
These are a few of my fa - vor - ite things.

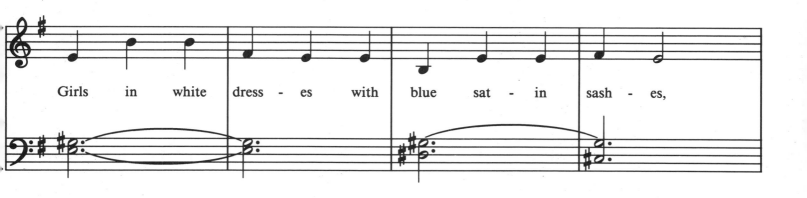

Girls in white dress - es with blue sat - in sash - es,

Snow - flakes that stay on my nose and eye - lash - es,

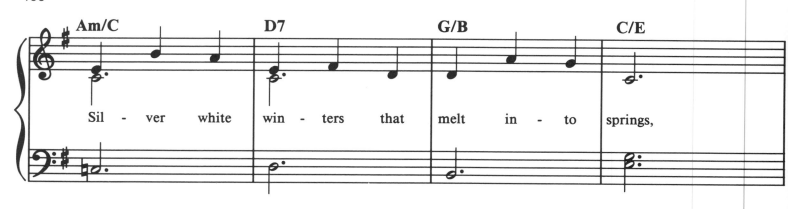

Sil - ver white win - ters that melt in - to springs,

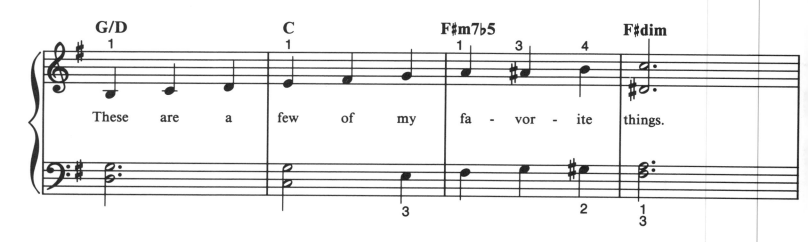

These are a few of my fa - vor - ite things.

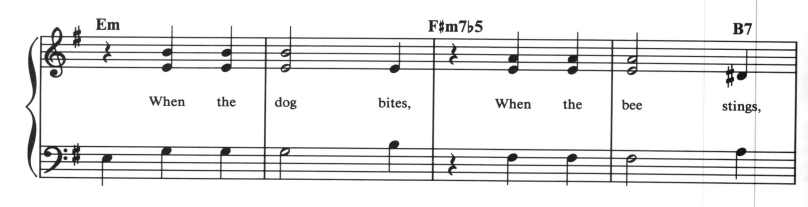

When the dog bites, When the bee stings,

When I'm feel - ing sad,

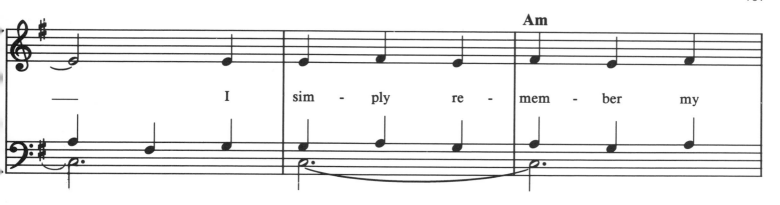

I sim - ply re - mem - ber my

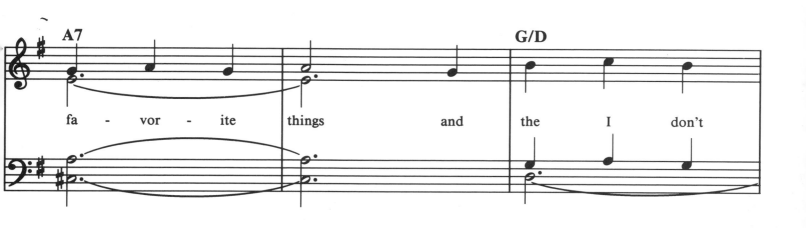

fa - vor - ite things and the I don't

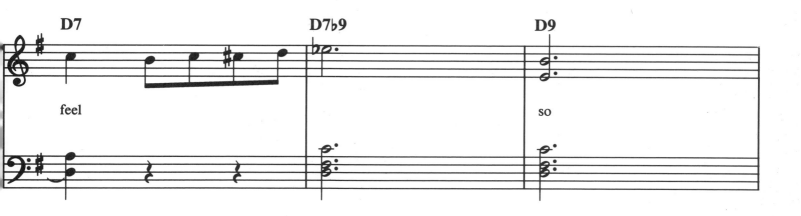

feel so

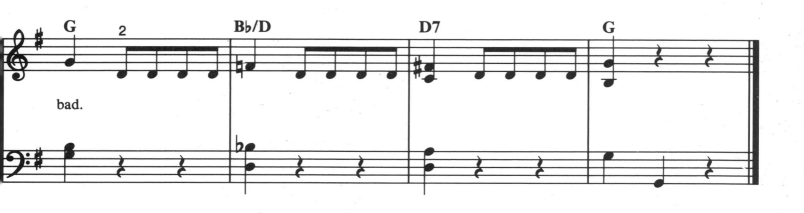

bad.

NEVER SMILE AT A CROCODILE

from Walt Disney's PETER PAN

Words by JACK LAWRENCE
Music by FRANK CHURCHILL

run, walk a - way; Say "Good- night" not "Good day."
rude, nev - er mock; Throw a kiss, not a rock. } Clear the aisle and nev- er smile at Mis- ter

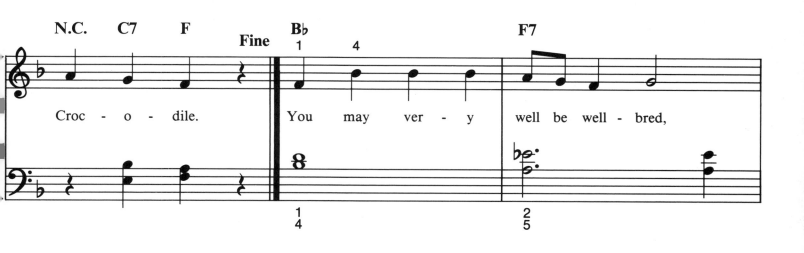

Croc — o — dile. You may ver - y well be well - bred,

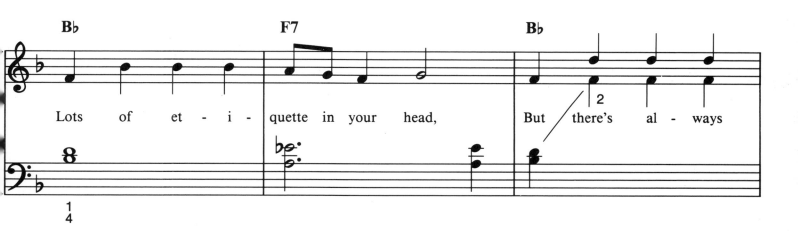

Lots of et - i - quette in your head, But there's al - ways

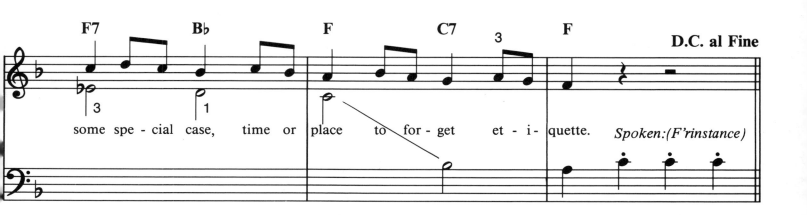

some spe - cial case, time or place to for - get et - i - quette. *Spoken:(F'rinstance)*

D.C. al Fine

OH WHERE, OH WHERE HAS MY LITTLE DOG GONE

American Words by SEP. WINNER
Traditional Melody

where, oh where can he be? Oh where, oh where has my

lit - tle dog gone? Oh where, oh where can he

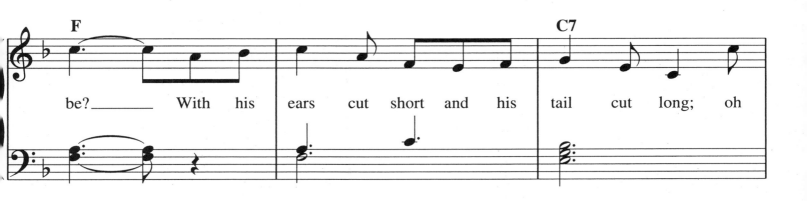

be?_____ With his ears cut short and his tail cut long; oh

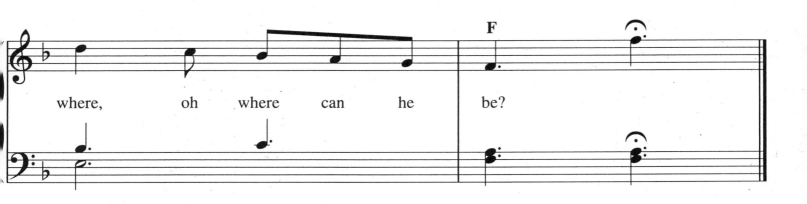

where, oh where can he be?

OLD MACDONALD HAD A FARM

Traditional

Here a quack, there a quack, ev-'ry-where a quack, quack. Old Mac-Don-ald

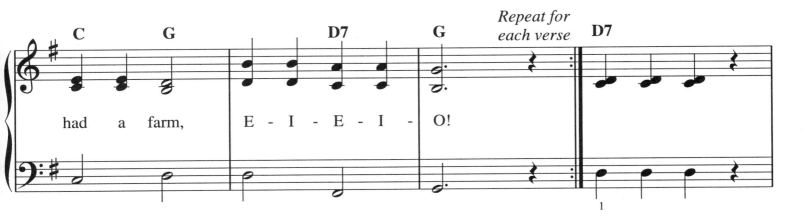

had a farm, E - I - E - I - O!

Repeat for each verse

Additional Lyrics

2. Old MacDonald Had a Farm,
E - I - E - I - O!
And on this farm he had a chick,
E - I - E - I - O!
With a chick, chick here
And a chick, chick there,
Here a chick, there a chick,
Everywhere a chick, chick
Old MacDonald Had a Farm,
E - I - E - I - O!

3. Other verses:

3. Cow - moo, moo
4. Dogs - bow, bow
5. Pigs - oink, oink
6. Rooster - cock-a-doodle, cock-a-doodle
7. Turkey - gobble, gobble
8. Cat - meow, meow
9. Horse - neigh, neigh
10. Donkey - hee-haw, hee-haw

ON TOP OF SPAGHETTI

Words and Music by
TOM GLAZER

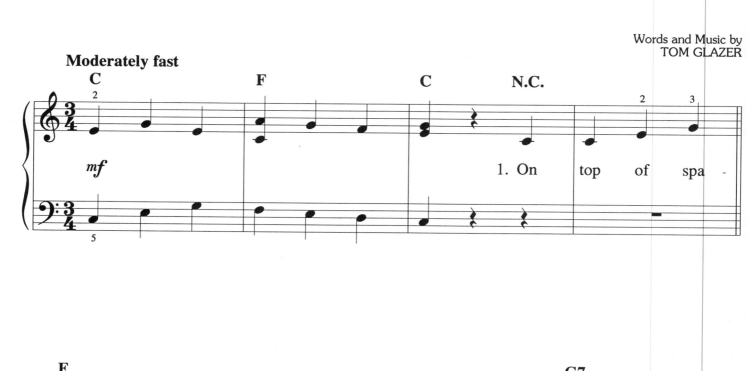

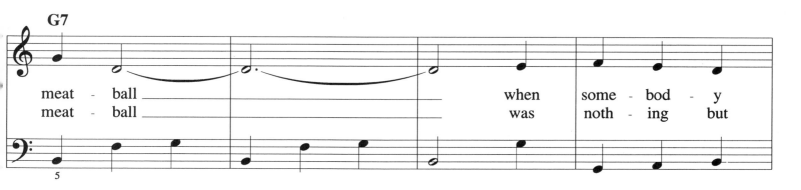

meat - ball _____ when some - bod - y
meat - ball _____ was noth - ing but

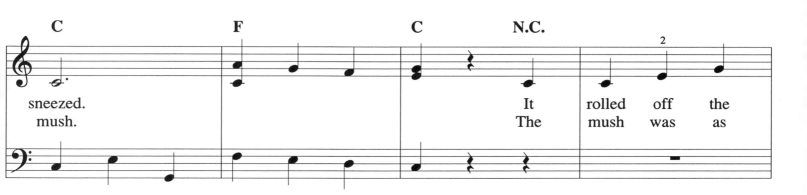

sneezed. It rolled off the
mush. The mush was as

ta - ble _____ and on - to the
tast - y _____ as tast - y could

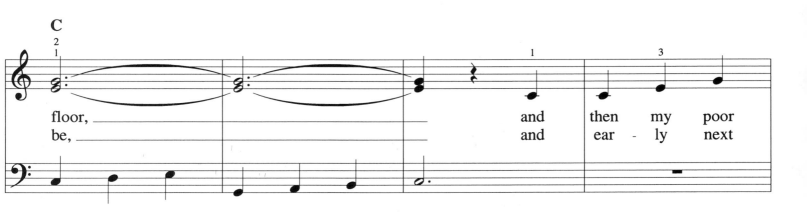

floor, _____ and then my poor
be, _____ and ear - ly next

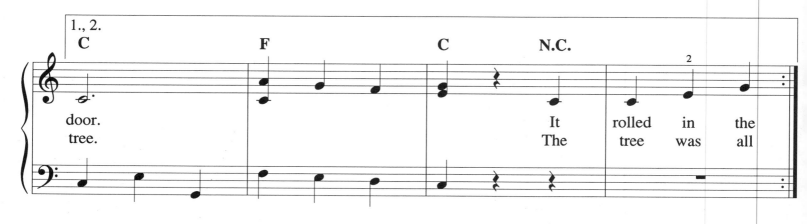

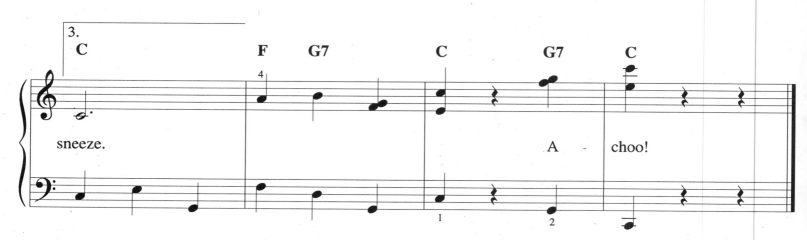

Additional Lyrics

3. The tree was all covered with beautiful moss;
   It grew lovely meatballs and tomato sauce.
   So if you eat spaghetti all covered with cheese,
   Hold on to your meatballs and don't ever sneeze.

ONE AND ONE ARE TWO

from MISTER ROGERS' NEIGHBORHOOD

Words and Music by
FRED ROGERS

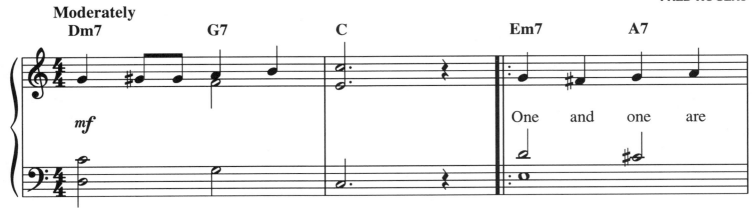

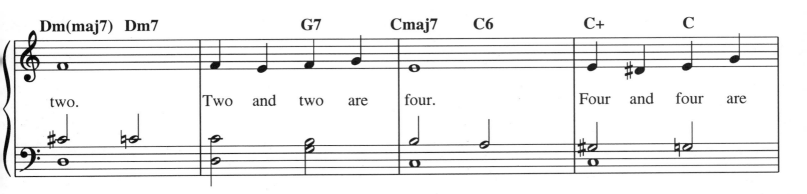

ONCE UPON A DREAM
from Walt Disney's SLEEPING BEAUTY

Words and Music by SAMMY FAIN and JACK LAWRENCE
Adapted from a Theme by TCHAIKOVSKY

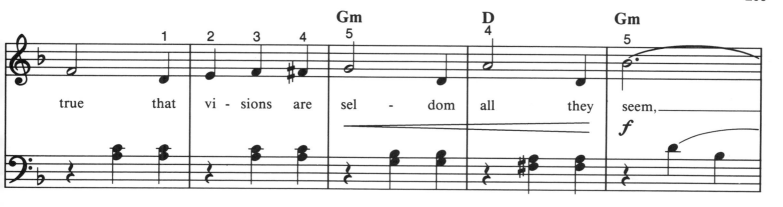

true that vi - sions are sel - dom all they seem,

But if I know you, I know what you'll

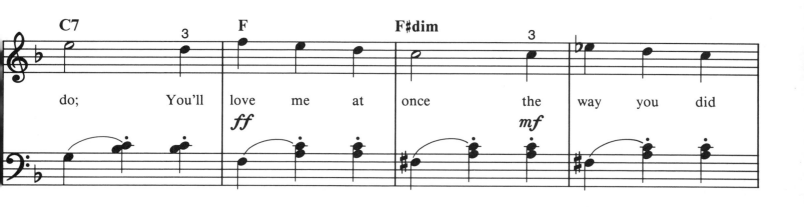

do; You'll love me at once the way you did

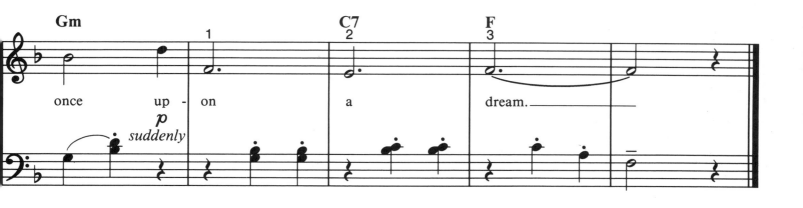

once up - on a dream.

OVER THE RIVER AND THROUGH THE WOODS

Traditional

O - ver the riv - er and through the woods, to
O - ver the riv - er and through the woods, to
O - ver the riv - er and through the woods, and

Grand - fa - ther's house we go. _____ The horse knows the way to
have a first - rate play. _____ Oh hear the bells ring,
straight thro' the barn - yard gate. _____ We seem __ to go ex -

car - ry the sleigh thro' the white and drift - ing
"Ting - a - ling - ling!" Hur - rah for Thanks - giv - ing
treme - ly slow, it is so hard to

PART OF YOUR WORLD

from Walt Disney's THE LITTLE MERMAID

Lyrics by HOWARD ASHMAN
Music by ALAN MENKEN

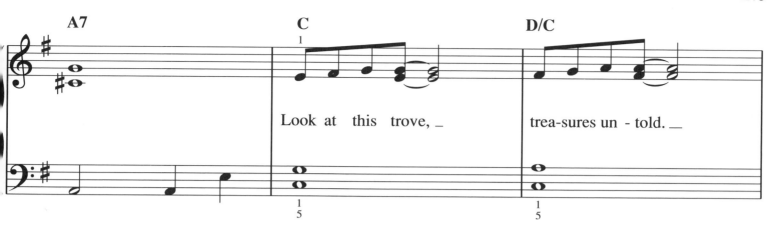

A7 | **C** | **D/C**

Look at this trove, _ trea-sures un - told. _

C | **D/C** | **Bm7**

How man-y won - ders can one cav-ern hold? Look-ing a - round _ here you'd

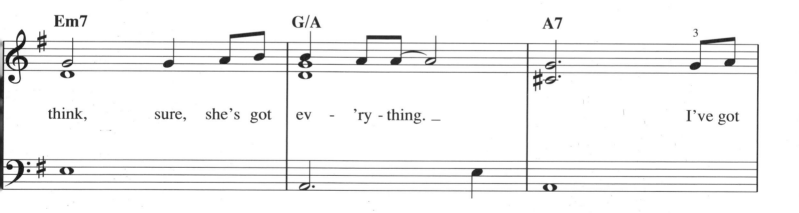

Em7 | **G/A** | **A7**

think, sure, she's got ev - 'ry - thing. _ I've got

Cmaj7 | **Bm** | **G/B** | **Em7**

gad - gets and giz - mos a - plen-ty. _____ I've got who - zits and what-zits ga -

feet.   Flip-pin' your fins _ you don't

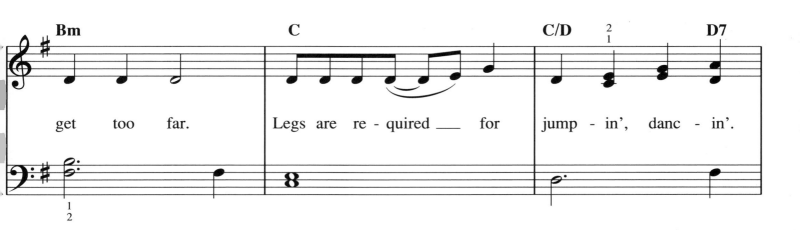

get   too   far.   Legs are re - quired ___ for   jump - in',   danc - in'.

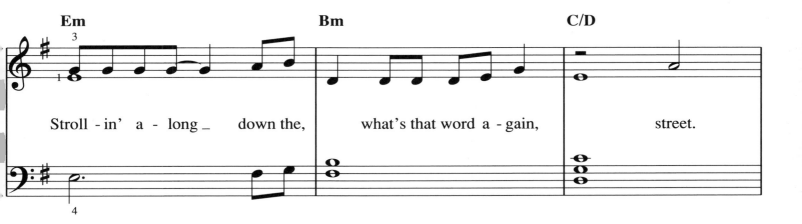

Stroll -in' a - long _ down the,   what's that word a - gain,   street.

Up where they   walk,   up where they   run,   up where they

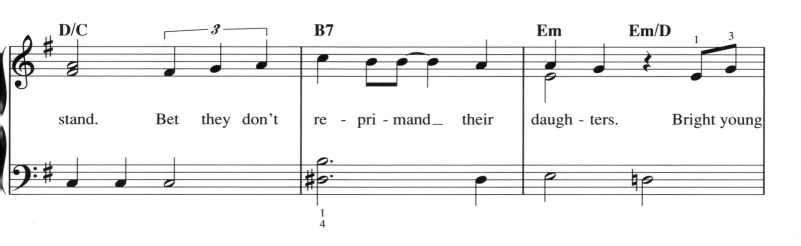

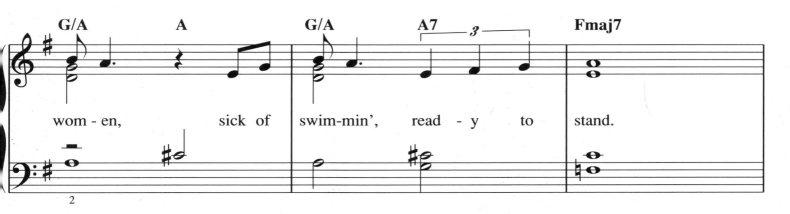

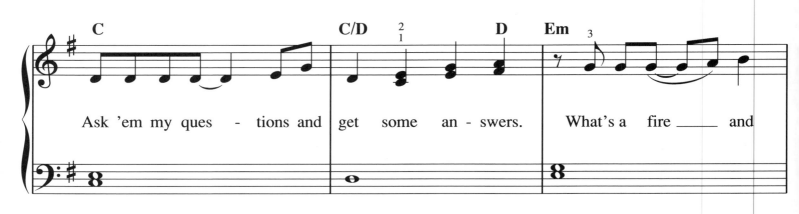

Ask 'em my ques - tions and get some an - swers. What's a fire _____ and

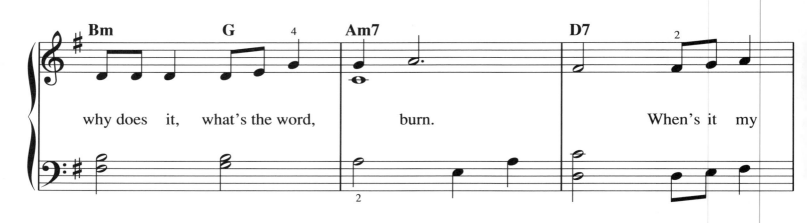

why does it, what's the word, burn. When's it my

turn? Would - n't I love, love to ex - plore that shore up a -

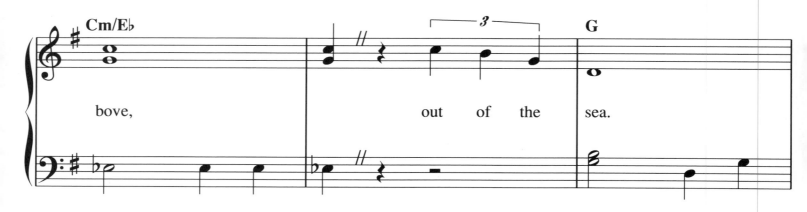

bove, out of the sea.

PETER COTTONTAIL

Words and Music by STEVE NELSON
and JACK ROLLINS

Moderato

Chorus

Easter Version
1. Here comes Pe - ter Cot - ton - tail, Hop - pin' down the
2. Here comes Pe - ter Cot - ton - tail, Hop - pin' down the

Year 'Round Version
1. Look at Pe - ter Cot - ton - tail, Hop - pin' down the
2. Lit - tle Pe - ter Cot - ton - tail, Hop - pin' down the

bun - ny trail,
bun - ny trail, Hip - pi - ty hop - pin' East - er's on it's
bun - ny trail, Look at him stop, and lis - ten to him
bun - ny trail, A rab - bit of dis - tinc - tion so they
Hap - pened to stop for car - rots on the

way.
say: "Try to do the Bring - in' ev - 'ry
say. He's the king of
way. Some - thing told him

221

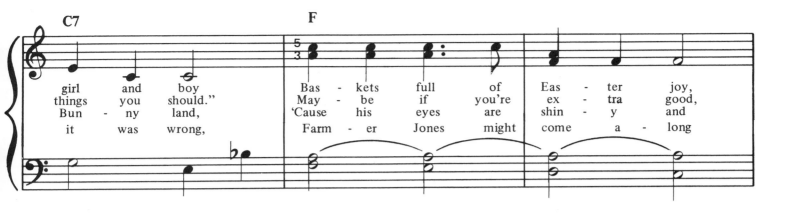

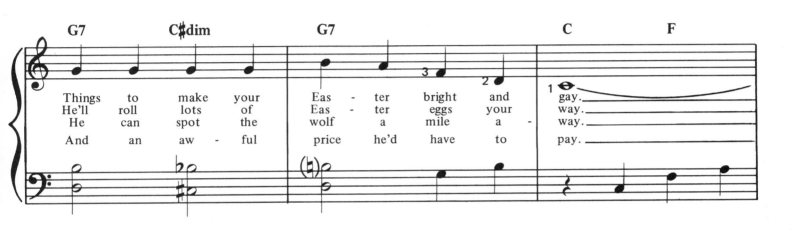

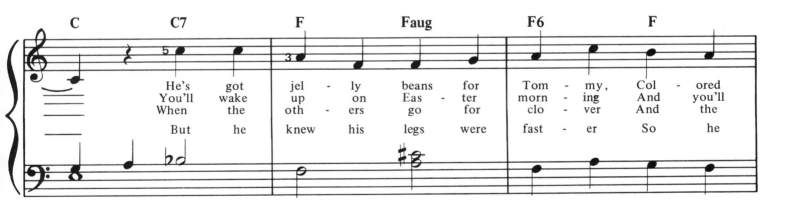

222

POLLY WOLLY DOODLE

Traditional American Minstrel Song

Bright, with humor

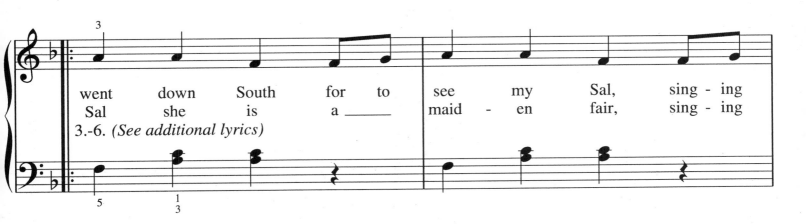

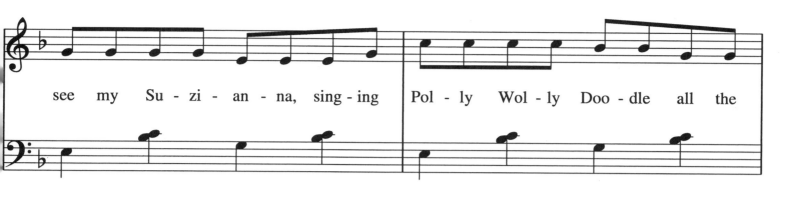

see my Su - zi - an - na, sing - ing Pol - ly Wol - ly Doo - dle all the

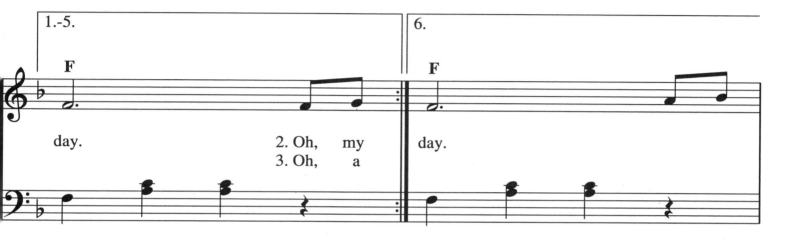

1.-5. F

day. 2. Oh, my
3. Oh, a

6. F

day.

C7

F

Additional Lyrics

3. Oh, a grasshopper sittin' on a railroad track,
   Singing Polly-Wolly Doodle all the day.
   A pickin' his teeth with a carpet tack,
   Singing Polly-Wolly Doodle all the day.
   To Chorus:

4. Oh, I went to bed, but it wasn't no use,
   Singing Polly-Wolly Doodle all the day.
   My feet stuck out like a chicken roost,
   Singing Polly-Wolly Doodle all the day.
   To Chorus:

5. Behind the barn down on my knees,
   Singing Polly-Wolly Doodle all the day.
   I thought I heard a chicken sneeze,
   Singing Polly-Wolly Doodle all the day.
   To Chorus:

6. He sneezed so hard with the whooping cough,
   Singing Polly-Wolly Doodle all the day.
   He sneezed his head and tail right off,
   Singing Polly-Wolly Doodle all the day.
   To Chorus:

POP GOES THE WEASEL

Traditional

Lyrics under the music:

All a-round the cob-bler's bench the mon-key chased the
Ru-fus has the whoop-ing cough, and Sal-ly has the

wea-sel. The mon-key thought 'twas all___ in fun.
mea-sles. And that's the way the doc-tor goes.

PUFF THE MAGIC DRAGON

Words by LEONARD LIPTON
Music by PETER YARROW

*After Verse 4, skip the Chorus and play Verse 5. Then play Chorus with last ending.

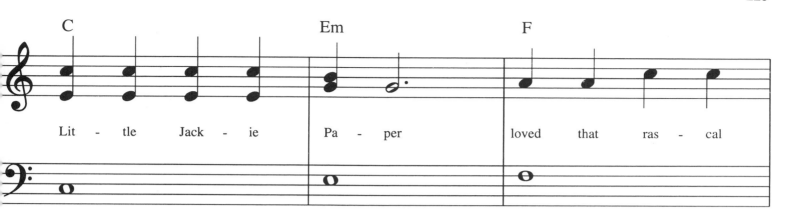

Lit - tle Jack - ie Pa - per loved that ras - cal

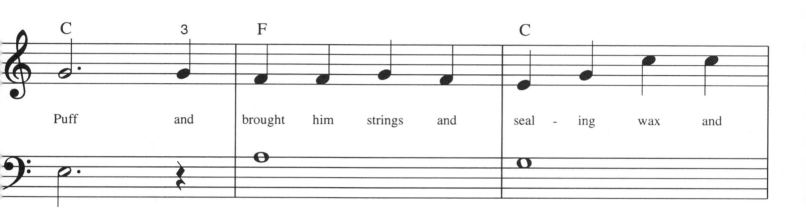

Puff and brought him strings and seal - ing wax and

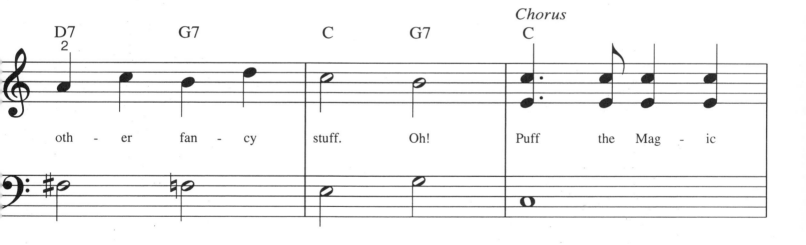

Chorus

oth - er fan - cy stuff. Oh! Puff the Mag - ic

Drag - on lived by the sea and

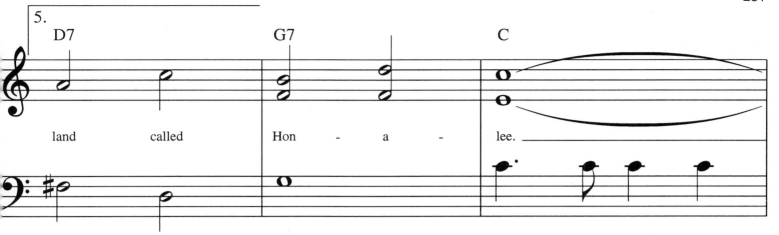

land   called   Hon - a - lee.

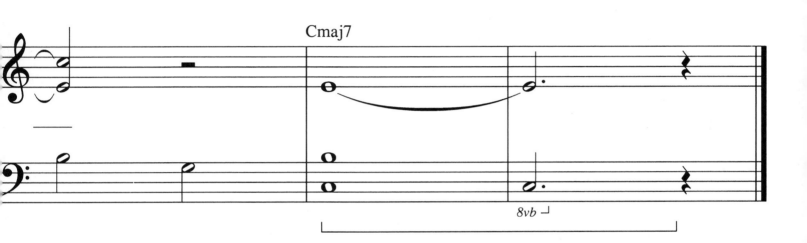

Cmaj7

8vb

Additional Lyrics

2. Together they would travel on a boat with billowed sail.
   Jackie kept a lookout perched on Puff's gigantic tail.
   Noble kings and princes would bow whene'er they came.
   Pirate ships would low'r their flag when Puff roared out his name. Oh! *(Chorus)*

3. A dragon lives forever, but not so little boys.
   Painted wings and giant rings make way for other toys.
   One gray night it happened, Jackie Paper came no more,
   And Puff that mighty dragon, he ceased his fearless roar. Oh! *(Chorus)*

4. His head was bent in sorrow, green tears fell like rain.
   Puff no longer went to play along the Cherry Lane.
   Without his lifelong friend, Puff could not be brave,
   So Puff that mighty dragon sadly slipped into his cave.

*THE RETURN OF PUFF

5. Puff the Magic Dragon danced down the Cherry Lane.
   He came upon a little girl, Julie Maple was her name.
   She'd heard that Puff had gone away, but that can never be.
   So together they went sailing to the land called Honalee. *(Chorus)*

THE RAINBOW CONNECTION

from THE MUPPET MOVIE

By PAUL WILLIAMS
and KENNETH L. ASCHER

with pedal

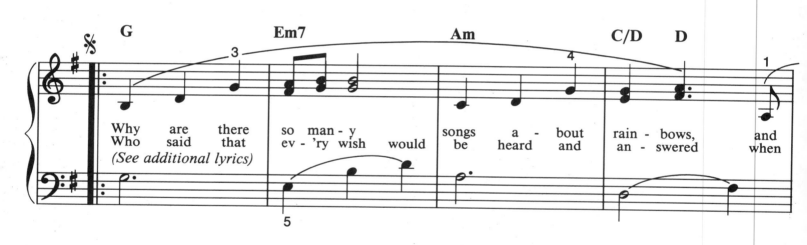

Why are there so man-y songs a-bout rain-bows, and
Who said that ev-'ry wish would be heard and an-swered when
(See additional lyrics)

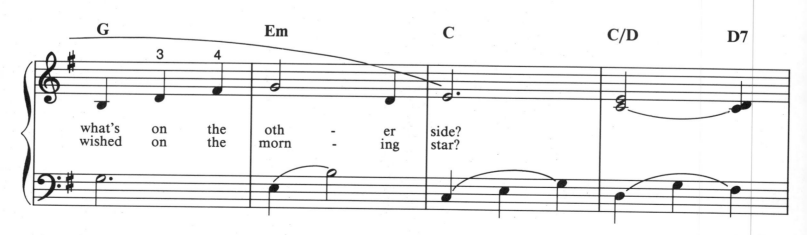

what's on the oth - er side?
wished on the morn - ing star?

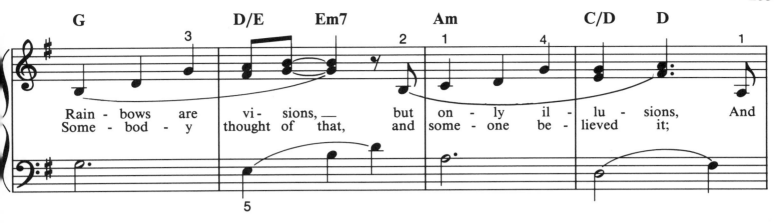

G   **D/E**   **Em7**   **Am**   **C/D**   **D**

Rain - bows are vi - sions, — but on - ly il - lu - sions, And
Some - bod - y thought of that, and some - one be - lieved it;

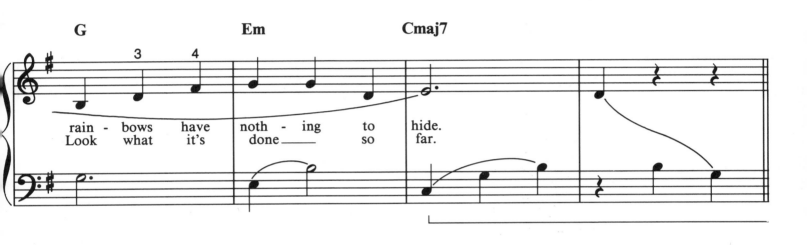

G   **Em**   **Cmaj7**

rain - bows have noth - ing to hide.
Look what it's done so far.

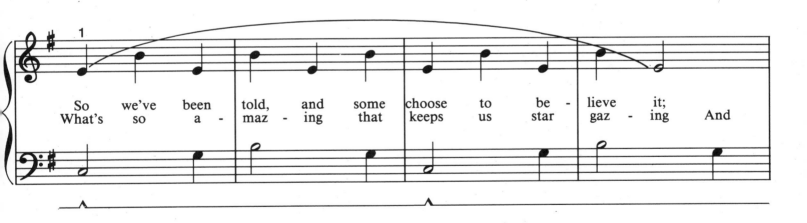

So we've been told, and some choose to be - lieve it;
What's so a - maz - ing that keeps us star - gaz - ing And

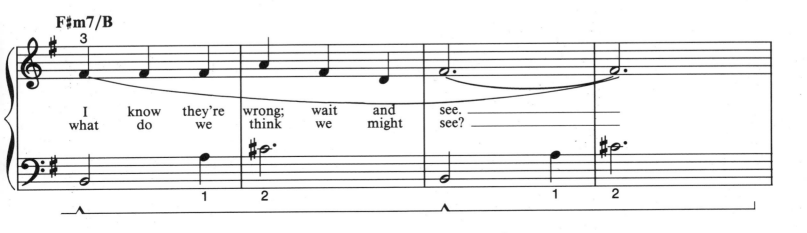

F♯m7/B

I know they're wrong; wait and see.
what do we think we might see?

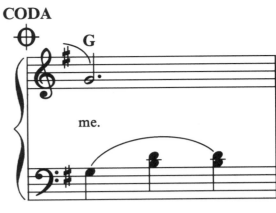

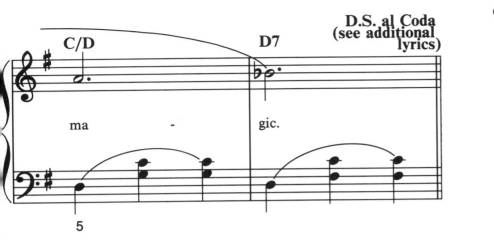

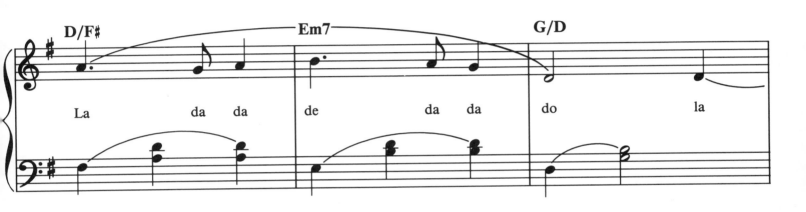

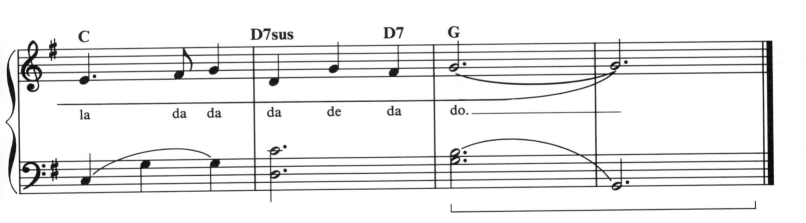

Additional Lyrics

Verse 3: Have you been half asleep and have you heard voices?
I've heard them calling my name.
Is this the sweet sound that calls the young sailors?
The voice might be one and the same.
I've heard it too many times to ignore it.
It's something that I'm s'posed to be.
Someday we'll find it,
The Rainbow Connection;
The lovers, the dreamers and (me.)
(To Coda)

RING AROUND THE ROSIE

Traditional

Rise, Sal - ly, rise, _____ wipe your weep - ing

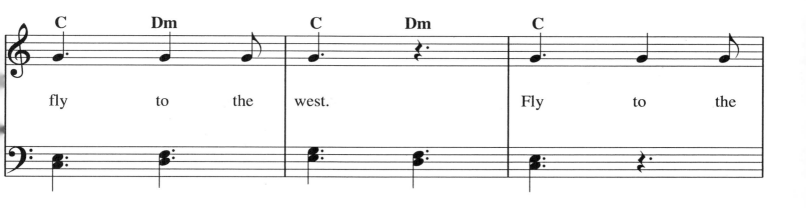

eyes; _____ fly to the east,

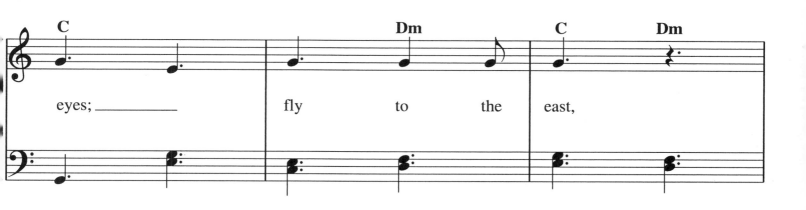

fly to the west. Fly to the

one that _____ you love best.

ROW, ROW, ROW YOUR BOAT

Traditional

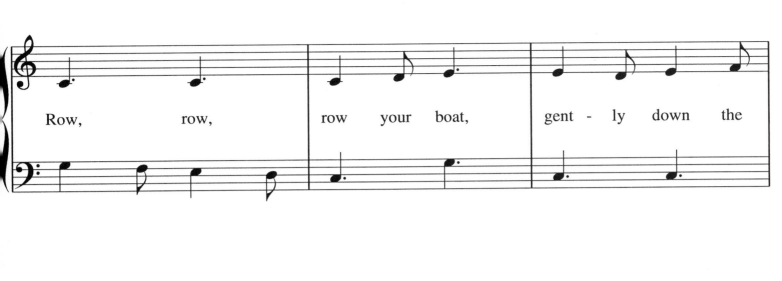

Row, row, row your boat, gent - ly down the

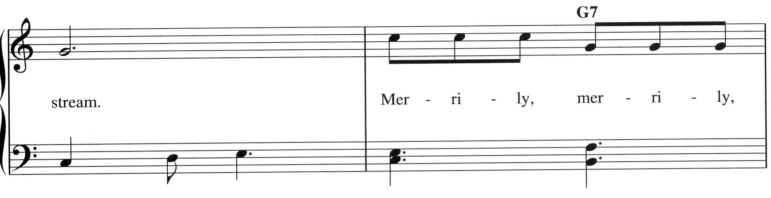

stream. Mer - ri - ly, mer - ri - ly,

mer - ri - ly, mer - ri - ly. Life is but a

dream.

RUBBER DUCKIE
from the Television Series SESAME STREET

Words and Music by
JEFF MOSS

Rub - ber Duck - ie, you're my ver - y best friend it's true.

Oh, ev - 'ry day when I make my way to the tub - by,

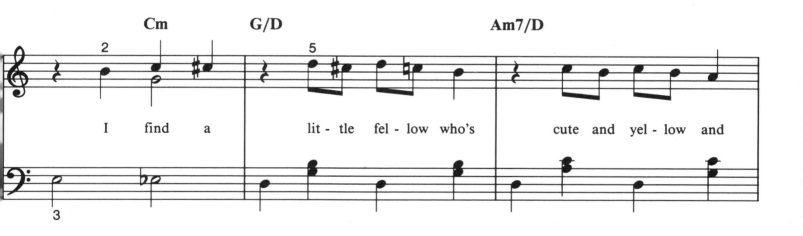

I find a lit - tle fel - low who's cute and yel - low and

chub - by, Rub - a - dub - dub - by. Rub - ber Duck - ie,

SAYING GOODBYE
from THE MUPPETS TAKE MANHATTAN

By JEFF MOSS

245

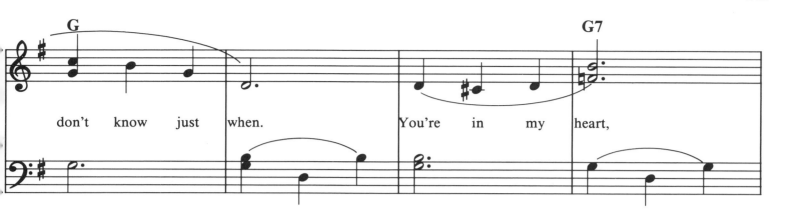

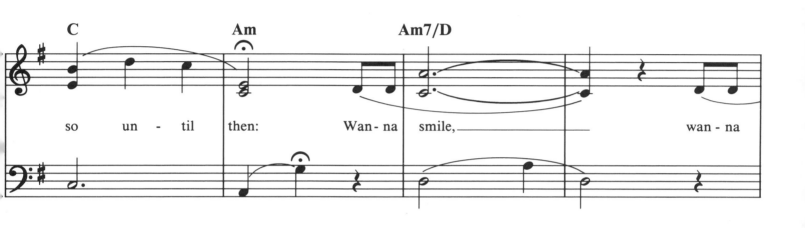

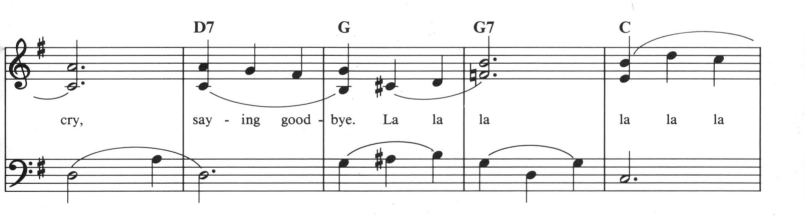

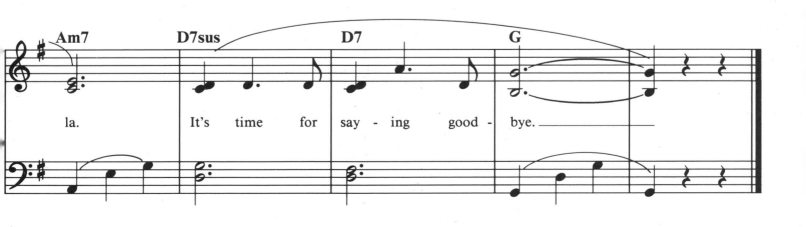

THE SIAMESE CAT SONG
from Walt Disney's LADY AND THE TRAMP

Words and Music by PEGGY LEE
and SONNY BURKE

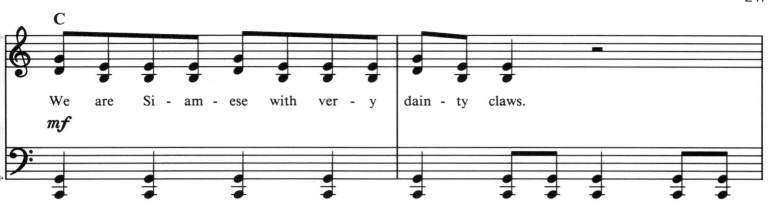

We are Si - am - ese with ver - y dain - ty claws.

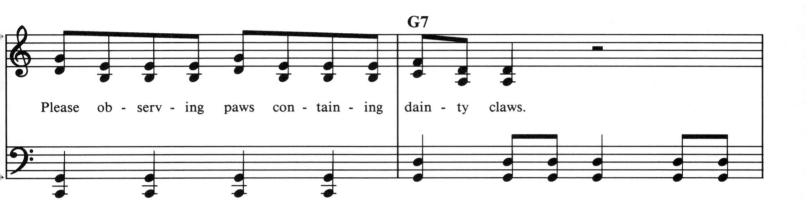

Please ob - serv - ing paws con - tain - ing dain - ty claws.

Now we look-in' o - ver our new dom - i - cile. If we like we stay for may - be

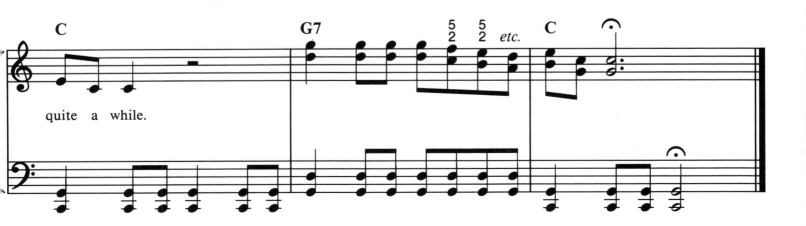

quite a while.

SING A SONG OF SIXPENCE

Traditional

SUPERCALIFRAGILISTIC-EXPIALIDOCIOUS

from Walt Disney's MARY POPPINS

Words and Music by RICHARD M. SHERMAN
and ROBERT B. SHERMAN

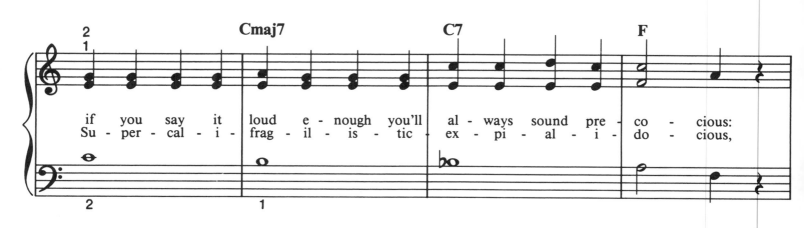

if you say it loud e - nough you'll al - ways sound pre - co - cious:
Su - per - cal - i - frag - il - is - tic - ex - pi - al - i - do - cious,

F#dim **C/G** **C#dim** **G7** **C** **Fine**

Su - per - cal - i - frag - il - is - tic - ex - pi - al - i - do - cious!
Su - per - cal - i - frag - il - is - tic - ex - pi - al - i - do - cious!

C **G7** **C**

L.H.
Um did - dle did - dle did - dle um did - dle ay! Um did - dle did - dle did - dle

G7 **C**

um did - dle ay! Be - cause I was a - fraid to speak when I was just a
So when the cat has got your tongue there's no need for dis -

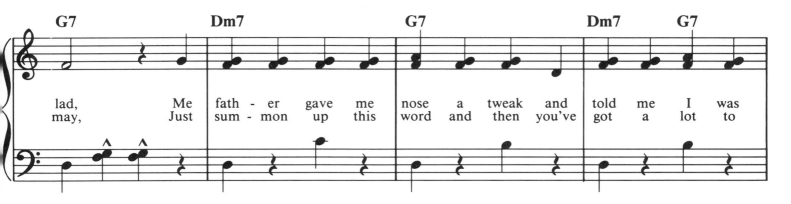

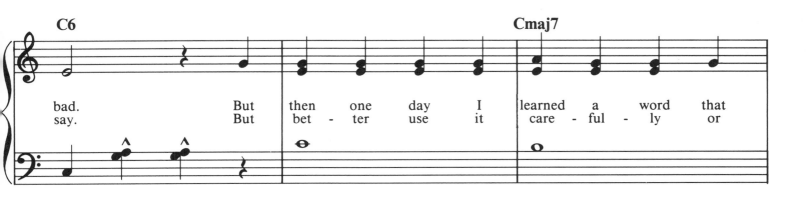

A SPOONFUL OF SUGAR
from Walt Disney's MARY POPPINS

Words and Music by RICHARD M. SHERMAN
and ROBERT B. SHERMAN

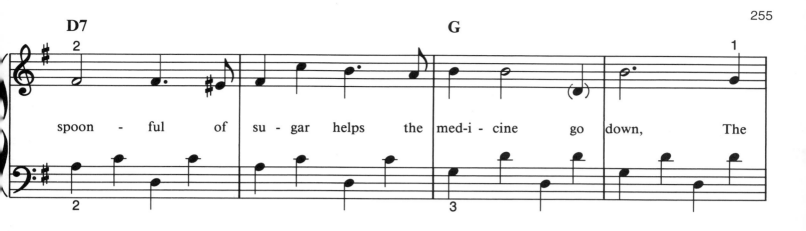

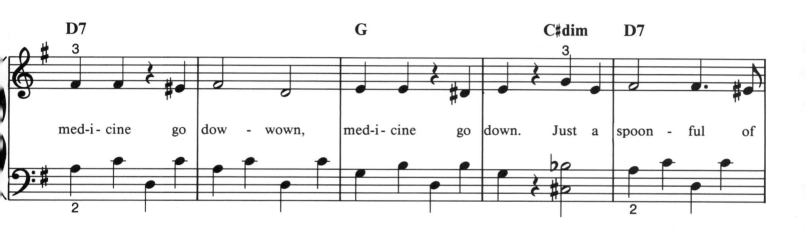

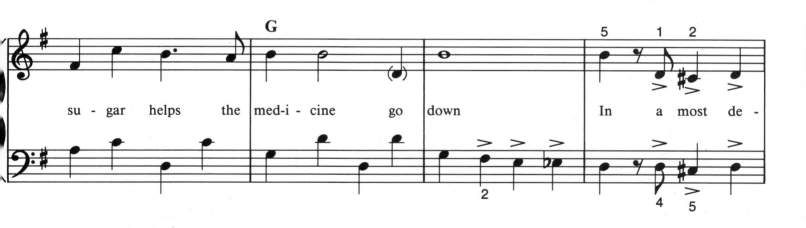

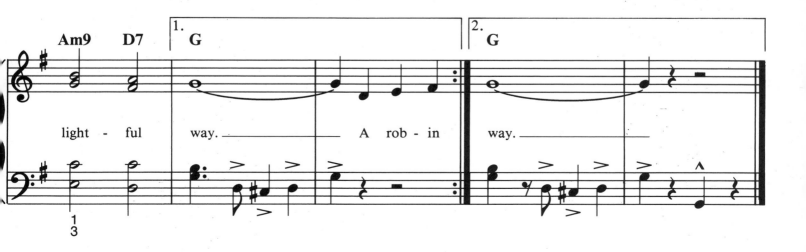

TAKE ME OUT TO THE BALL GAME

Words by JACK NORWORTH
Music by ALBERT VON TILZER

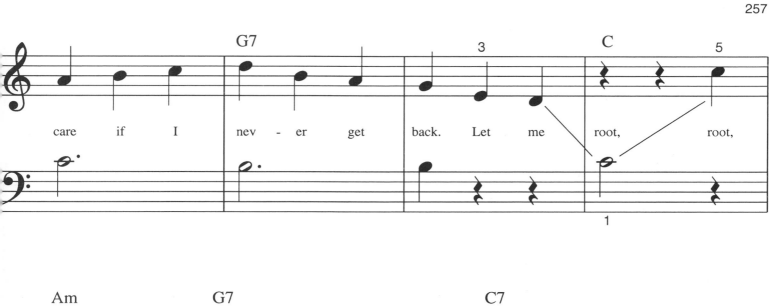

care if I nev - er get back. Let me root, root,

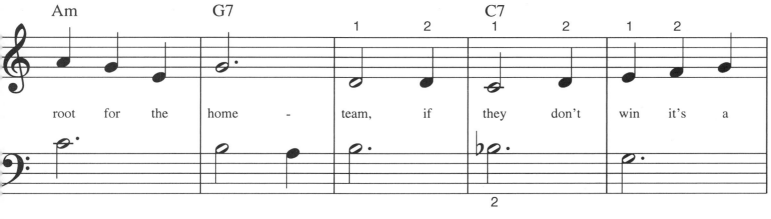

root for the home - team, if they don't win it's a

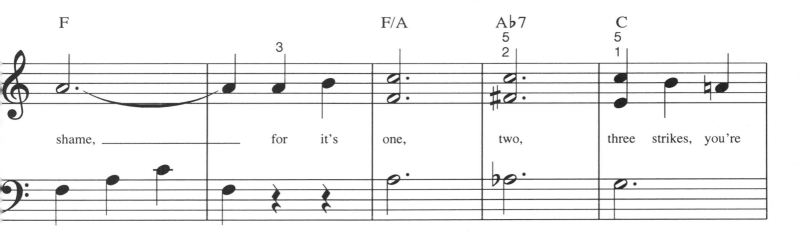

shame, _____ for it's one, two, three strikes, you're

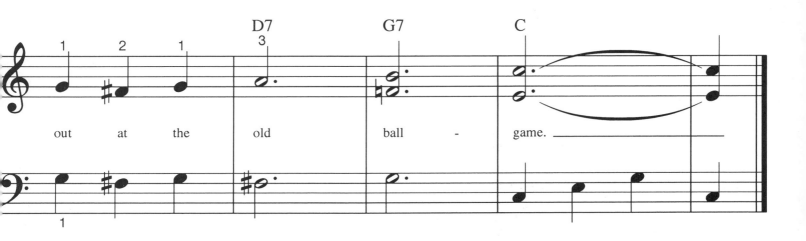

out at the old ball - game. _____

THERE'S A HOLE IN THE BOTTOM OF THE SEA

Traditional

Bright, with a shuffle (♩♩ **played as** ♩ ♪)

*See explanation with additional lyrics

hole,   there's a hole.   There's a   hole   in the bot - tom of the

sea.   There's a

eye   on the flea, there's a   flea   on the wing, there's a   wing   on the fly, there's a

fly   on the frog, there's a   frog   on the bump, there's a bump on the log, there's a

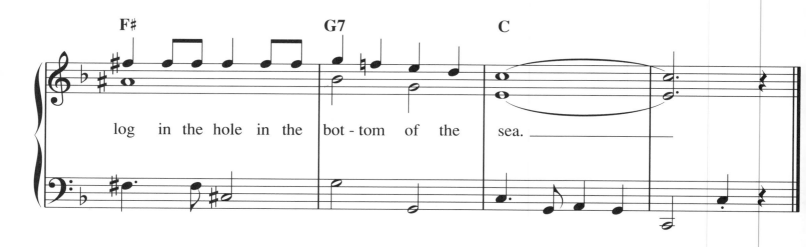

log in the hole in the bot - tom of the sea. _____

Additional Lyrics

*(For each new verse, add 2 extra beats (keep repeating the
first two beats) to the bars that are marked with an asterisk.)*
(Extra beats are underlined below.)

2. There's a <u>log in the</u> hole in the bottom of the sea.
   There's a <u>log in the</u> hole in the bottom of the sea.
   There's a log, there's a log.
   There's a <u>log in the</u> hole in the bottom of the sea.

3. There's a <u>bump on the log in the</u> hole in the bottom of the sea.
   There's a <u>bump on the log in the</u> hole in the bottom of the sea.
   There's a bump, there's a bump.
   There's a <u>bump on the log in the</u> hole in the bottom of the sea.

4. There's a <u>frog on the bump on the log in the</u>
   hole in the bottom of the sea.
   There's a <u>frog on the bump on the log in the</u>
   hole in the bottom of the sea.
   There's a frog, there's a frog.
   There's a<u> frog on the bump on the log in the</u>
   hole in the bottom of the sea.

5. There's a <u>fly on the frog on the bump on the log in the</u>
   hole in the bottom of the sea.
   There's a <u>fly on the frog on the bump on the log in the</u>
   hole in the bottom of the sea.
   There's a fly, there's a fly.
   There's a <u>fly on the frog on the bump on the log in the</u>
   hole in the bottom of the sea.

6. There's a <u>wing on the fly on the frog on the bump on</u>
   the <u>log in the</u> hole in the bottom of the sea.
   There's a <u>wing on the fly on the frog on the bump on</u>
   the <u>log in the</u> hole in the bottom of the sea.
   There's a wing, there's a wing.
   There's a <u>wing on the fly on the frog on the bump on</u>
   the <u>log in the</u> hole in the bottom of the sea.

7. There's a <u>flea on the wing of the fly on the frog on the</u>
   <u>bump on the log</u> in the hole in the bottom of the sea.
   There's a <u>flea on the wing of the fly on the frog on the</u>
   <u>bump on the log</u> in the hole in the bottom of the sea.
   There's a flea, there's a flea.
   There's a <u>flea on the wing of the fly on the frog on the</u>
   <u>bump on the log</u> in the hole in the bottom of the sea.

8. There's an <u>eye on the flea on the wing of the fly on the frog on the bump on the log in the</u> hole in the bottom of the sea.
   There's an <u>eye on the flea on the wing of the fly on the frog on the bump on the log in the</u> hole in the bottom of the sea.
   There's a wing, there's a wing.
   There's an <u>eye on the flea on the wing of the fly on the frog on the bump on the log in the</u> hole in the bottom of the sea.

(ENDING)

There's an eye on the flea on the wing,
There's a wing on the fly on the frog,
There's a frog on the bump, there's a bump on the log,
There's a log in the hoe in the bottom of the sea.

THERE'S A HOLE IN THE BUCKET

Traditional

Additional Lyrics

2. Well, fix it, dear Henry, etc.
3. With what shall I fix it, dear Liza, etc.
4. With a straw, dear Henry, etc.
5. But the straw is too long, dear Liza, etc.
6. Then cut it, dear Henry, etc.
7. With what shall I cut it, dear Liza, etc.
8. With a knife, dear Henry, etc.
9. But the knife is too dull, dear Liza, etc.
10. Then sharpen it, dear Henry, etc.
11. With what shall I sharpen it, dear Liza, etc.
12. With a stone, dear Henry, etc.
13. But the stone is too dry, dear Liza, etc.
14. Then wet it, dear Henry, etc.
15. With what shall I wet it, dear Liza, etc.
16. With water, dear Henry, etc.
17. In what shall I carry it, dear Liza, etc.
18. In a bucket, dear Henry, etc.
19. There's a hole in my bucket, dear Liza, etc.

THIS LITTLE LIGHT OF MINE

African-American Spiritual

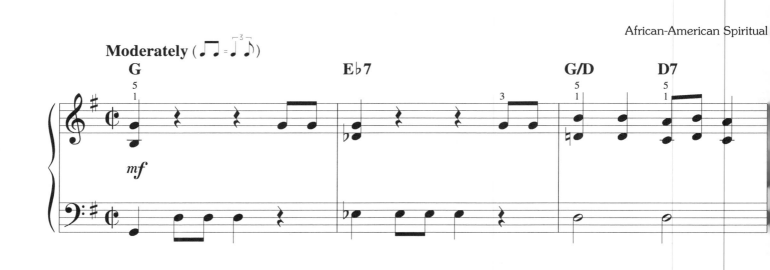

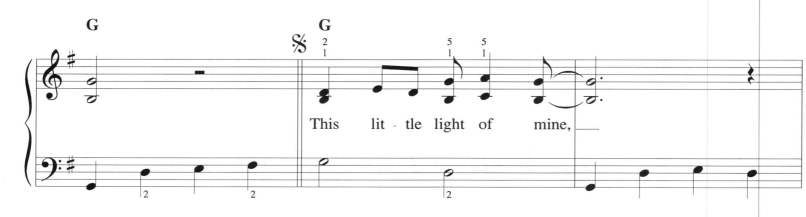

This lit-tle light of mine,___

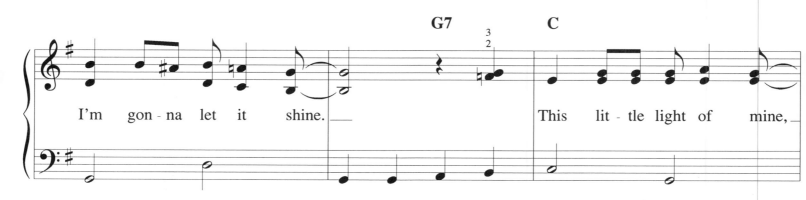

I'm gon-na let it shine.___   This lit-tle light of mine,___

watch and pray, on Sat-ur-day told me just what to say, on

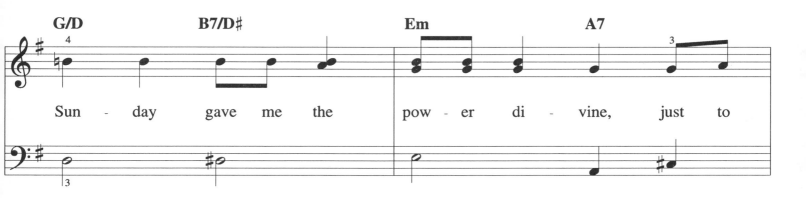

Sun - day gave me the pow - er di - vine, just to

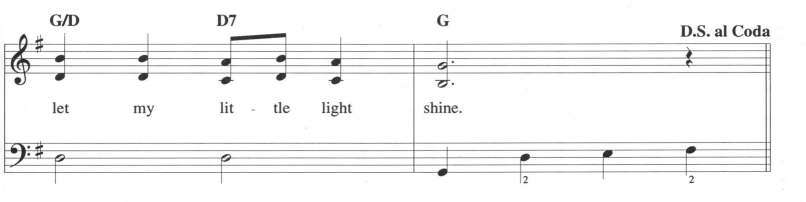

let my lit - tle light shine.

D.S. al Coda

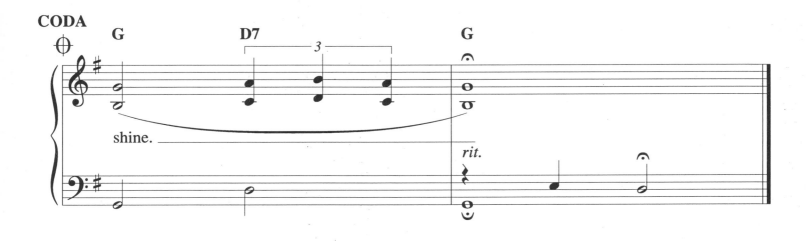

CODA

shine.

rit.

THIS OLD MAN

Traditional

This old man, he played one. He played knick - knack

on my drum, with a knick - knack pad - dy - whack, give the dog a bone.

This old man came roll - ing home.

2. This old man, he played two.
3.-10. *(See additional lyrics)*

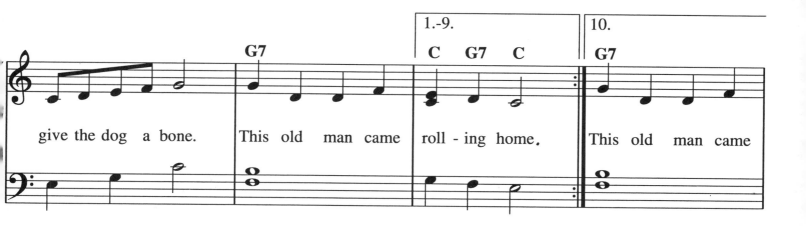

Additional Lyrics

3. This old man, he played three,
   He played knick-knack on my knee. *(Chorus)*

4. This old man, he played four,
   He played knick-knack on my door. *(Chorus)*

5. This old man, he played five,
   He played knick-knack on my hive. *(Chorus)*

6. This old man, he played six,
   He played knick-knack on my sticks. *(Chorus)*

7. This old man, he played seven,
   He played knick-knack up to heaven. *(Chorus)*

8. This old man, he played eight,
   He played knick-knack at the gate. *(Chorus)*

9. This old man, he played nine,
   He played knick-knack on my line. *(Chorus)*

10. This old man, he played ten,
    He played knick-knack over again. *(Chorus)*

THREE BLIND MICE

Traditional

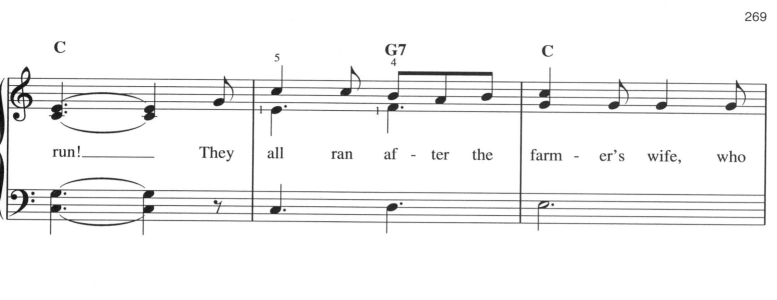

run!_____ They all ran af - ter the farm - er's wife, who

cut off their tails with a carv - ing knife. Did

you ev - er see such a sight in your life as three blind

mice.

TOMORROW
from the Musical Production ANNIE

Lyric by MARTIN CHARNIN
Music by CHARLES STROUSE

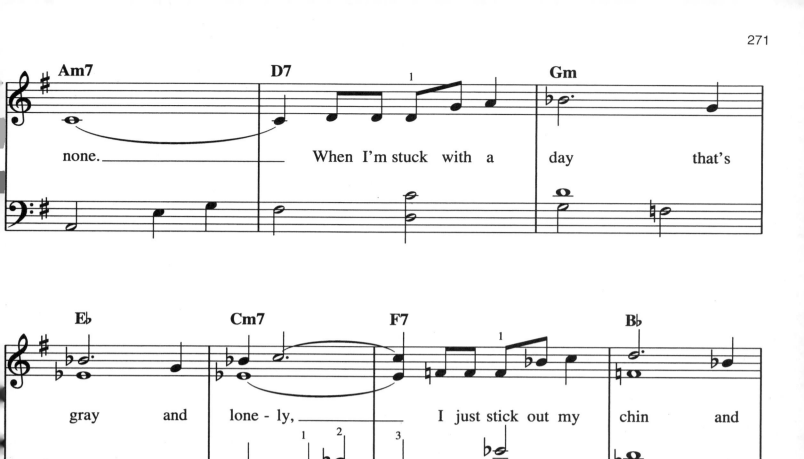

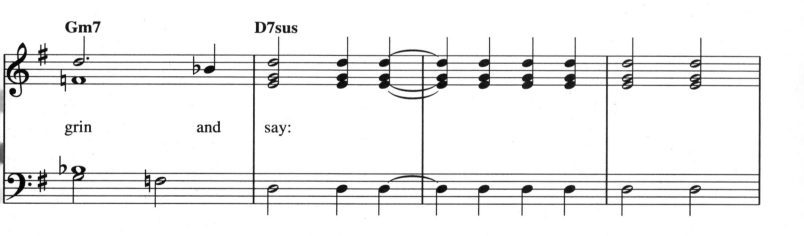

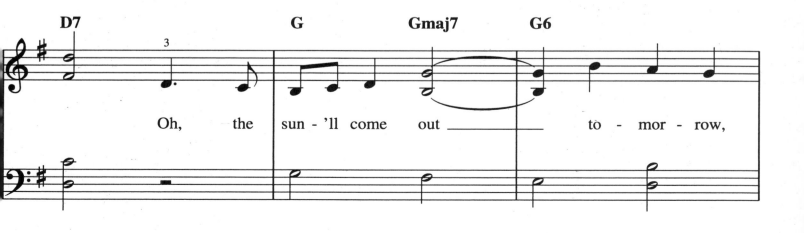

THE UNBIRTHDAY SONG
from Walt Disney's ALICE IN WONDERLAND

Words and Music by MACK DAVID,
AL HOFFMAN and JERRY LIVINGSTON

275

TWINKLE, TWINKLE LITTLE STAR

Traditional

Twin - kle, twin - kle,
(See additional lyrics) lit - tle star, How I won - der

what you are! Up a - bove the world so high,

Like a dia - mond in the sky. Twin - kle, twin - kle,

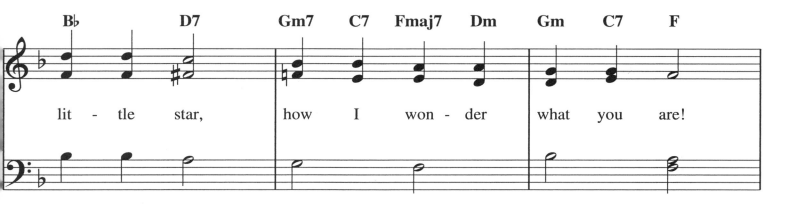

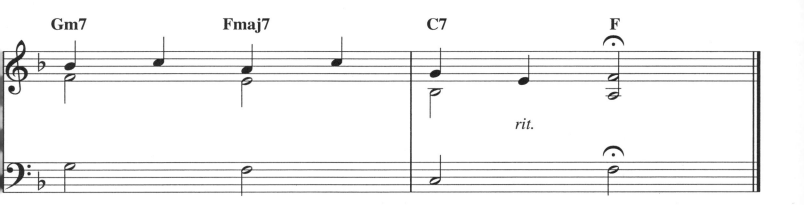

Additional Lyrics

THE ALPHABET SONG

A B C D E F G,
H I J K LMNOP,
Q R S, T U V,
W, X, Y, and Z.
Now you know my ABCs;
next time won't you sing with me?

BAA, BAA, BLACK SHEEP

Baa, baa, black sheep;
have you any wool?
"Yes, sir; yes sir.
Three bags full.
One for my master,
one for my dame,
one for the little boy
who lies in the lane."

Baa, baa, black sheep;
have you any wool?
"Yes, sir; yes sir.
Three bags full.

WHEN YOU WISH UPON A STAR

from Walt Disney's PINOCCHIO

Words by NED WASHINGTON
Music by LEIGH HARLINE

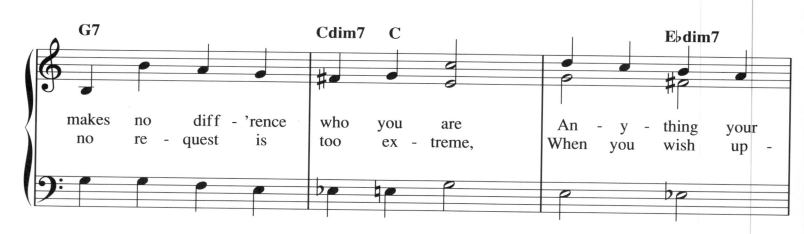

heart de - sires will come to you. ____

on a star as dream - ers

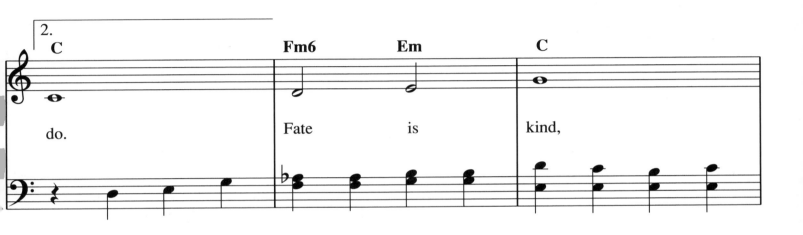

do. Fate is kind,

She brings to those who love

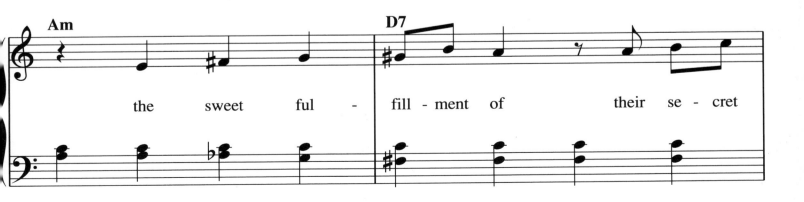

the sweet ful - fill - ment of their se - cret

WHO'S AFRAID OF THE BIG BAD WOLF?

from Walt Disney's THREE LITTLE PIGS

Words and Music by FRANK CHURCHILL
Additional Lyric by ANN RONELL

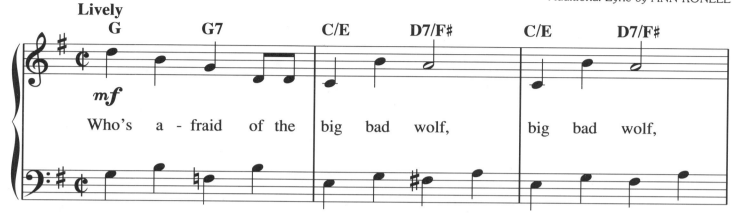

WHISTLE WHILE YOU WORK

from Walt Disney's SNOW WHITE AND THE SEVEN DWARFS

Words by LARRY MOREY
Music by FRANK CHURCHILL

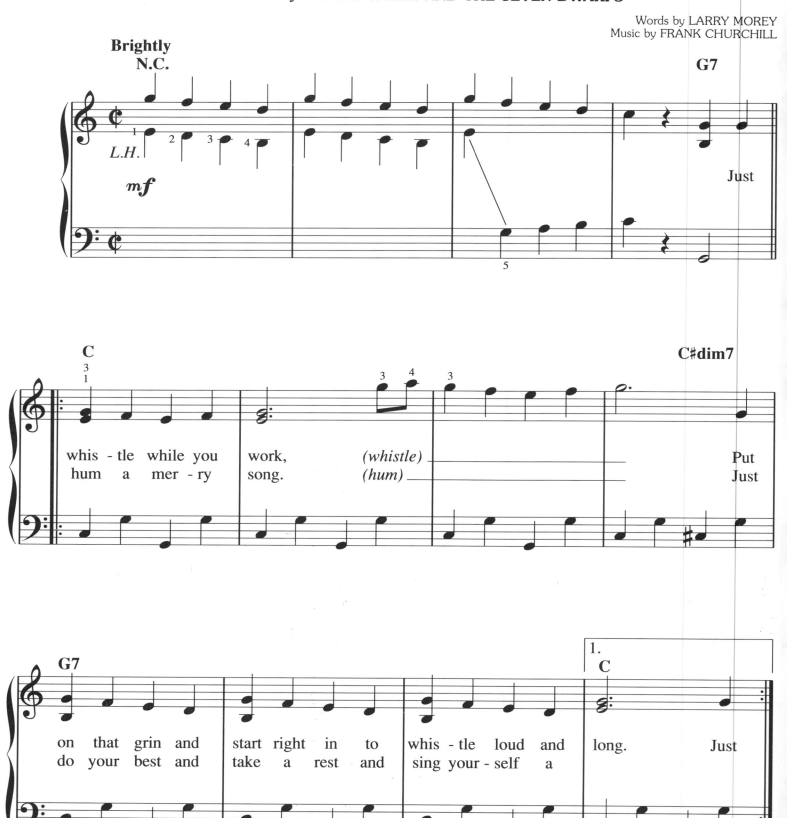

song. When there's too much to do don't let it both - er

you; For - get your trou - bles, try to be just like a cheer - ful

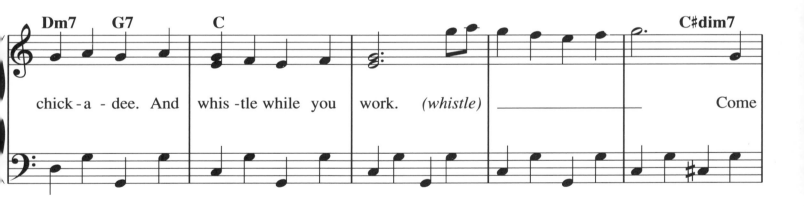

chick - a - dee. And whis - tle while you work. *(whistle)* _____ Come

on get smart, tune up and start to whis - tle while you work.

A WHOLE NEW WORLD

from Walt Disney's ALADDIN

Music by ALAN MENKEN
Lyrics by TIM RICE

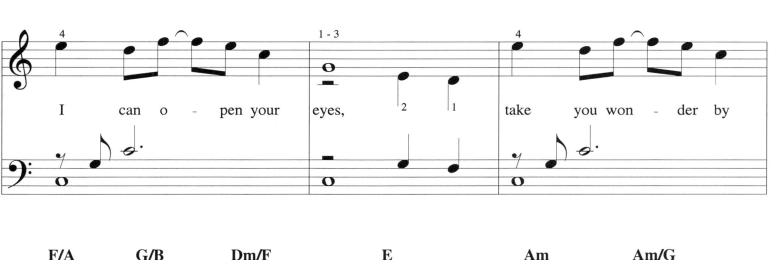

*♩♩♩ = a quarter-note triplet played over the time of two quarter notes.

WINNIE THE POOH

from Walt Disney's THE MANY ADVENTURES OF WINNIE THE POOH

Words and Music by RICHARD M. SHERMAN
and ROBERT B. SHERMAN

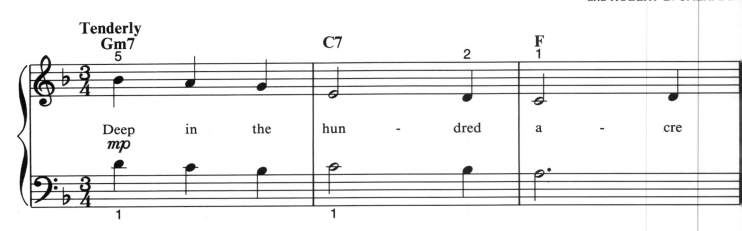

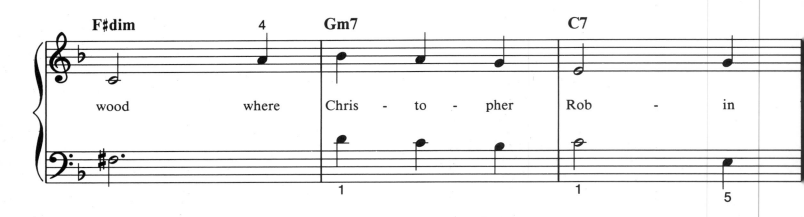

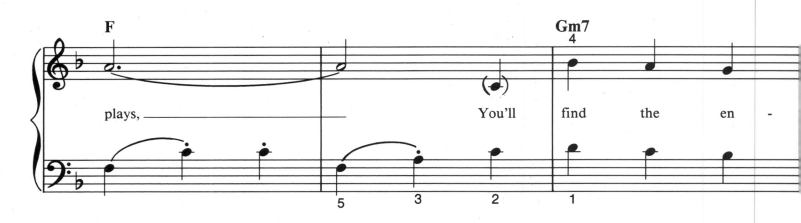

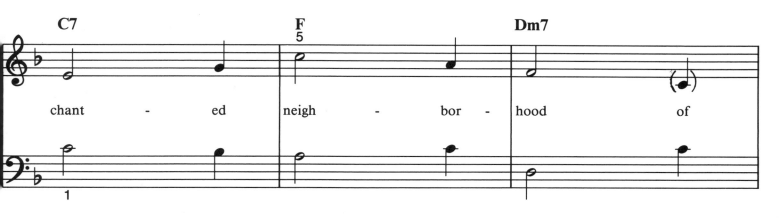

chant - ed neigh - bor - hood of

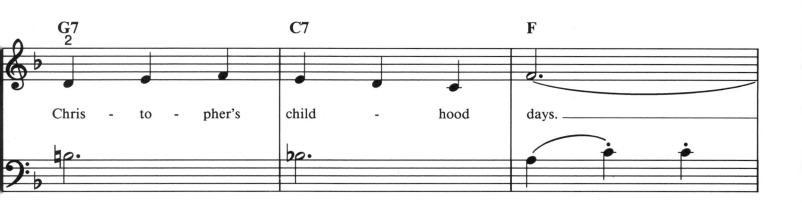

Chris - to - pher's child - hood days. ____

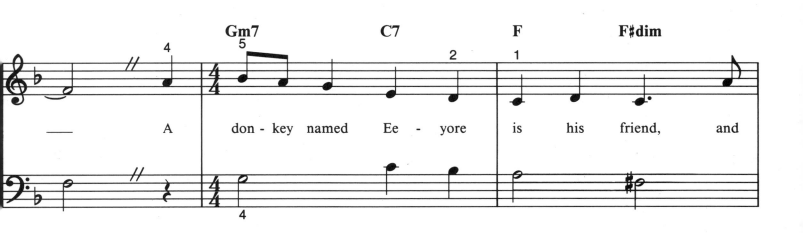

____ A don - key named Ee - yore is his friend, and

Kan - ga and lit - tle Roo; There's Rab - bit, there's Pig - let

YANKEE DOODLE

Traditional

WON'T YOU BE MY NEIGHBOR?
(It's a Beautiful Day in This Neighborhood)
from MISTER ROGERS' NEIGHBORHOOD

Words and Music by
FRED ROGERS

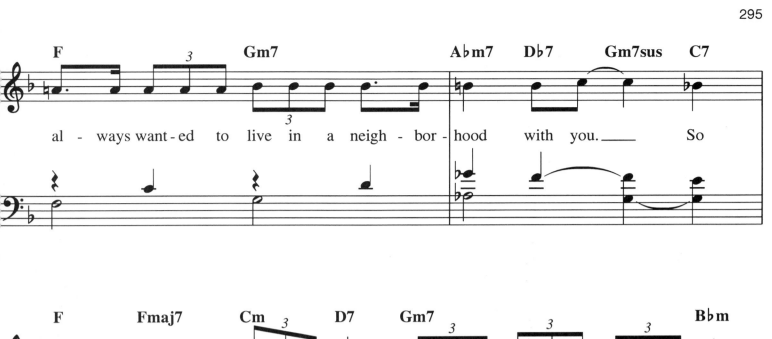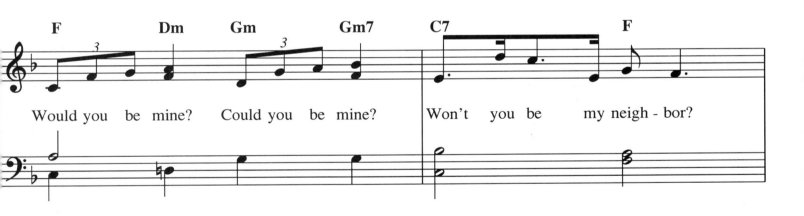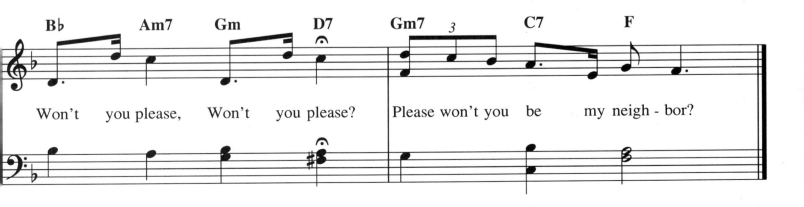

ZACCHAEUS

Traditional

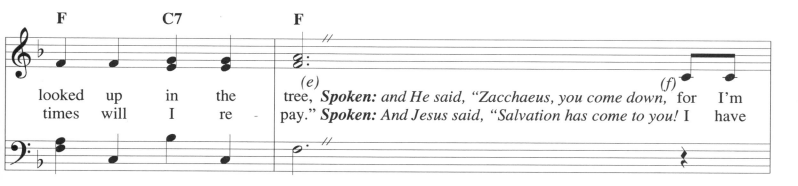

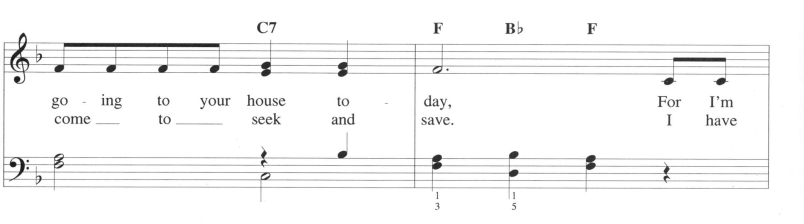

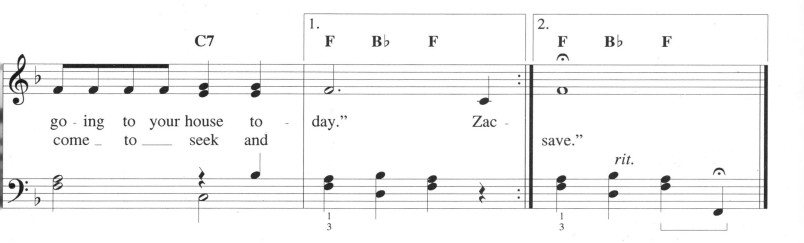

Motions for Verse 1:

(a) *Hands in front, right palm raised above left palm.*
(b) *Alternate hands in climbing motion.*
(c) *Shade eyes with right hand and look down.*
(d) *Shade eyes with right hand and look up.*
(e) *Speak these words while looking up and beckoning with hand.*
(f) *Clap hands on beats 1 and 3 until end of Verse 1.*

ZIP-A-DEE-DOO-DAH

from Walt Disney's SONG OF THE SOUTH

Words by RAY GILBERT
Music by ALLIE WRUBEL

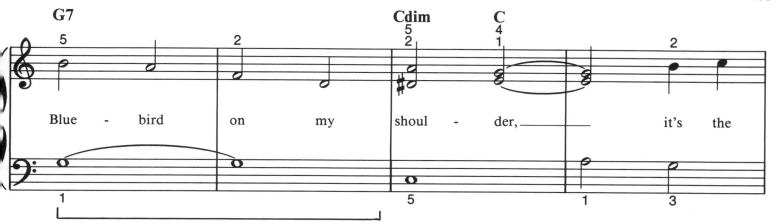

Blue - bird on my shoul - der, _____ it's the

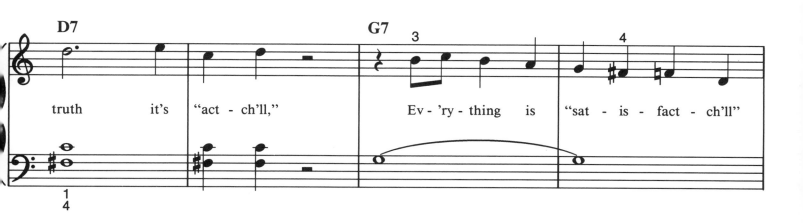

truth it's "act - ch'll," Ev - 'ry - thing is "sat - is - fact - ch'll"

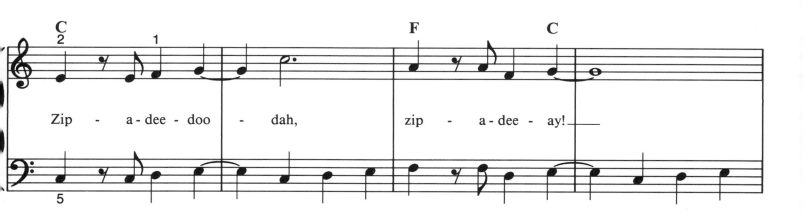

Zip - a - dee - doo - dah, zip - a - dee - ay! _____

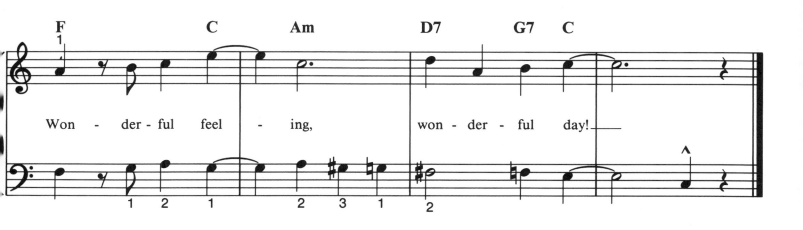

Won - der - ful feel - ing, won - der - ful day! _____

YELLOW SUBMARINE

Words and Music by JOHN LENNON and PAUL McCARTNEY

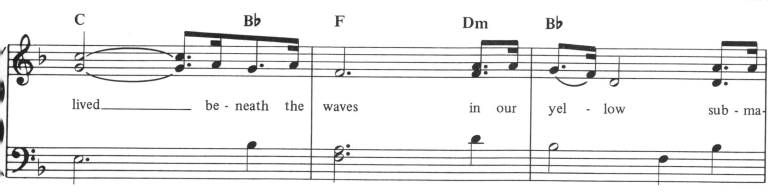

lived_____ be - neath the waves in our yel - low sub - ma-

rine. We all live in a yel - low sub - ma - rine,

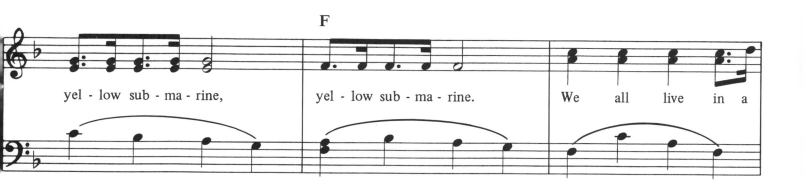

yel - low sub - ma - rine, yel - low sub - ma - rine. We all live in a

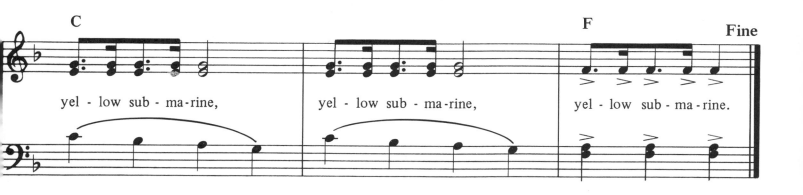

yel - low sub - ma - rine, yel - low sub - ma - rine, yel - low sub - ma - rine.

And our friends_____ are all on board, man - y
As we live_____ a life of ease, ev - 'ry

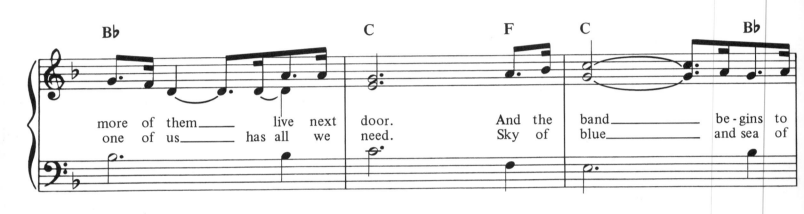

more of them____ live next door. And the band____ be - gins to
one of us____ has all we need. Sky of blue____ and sea of

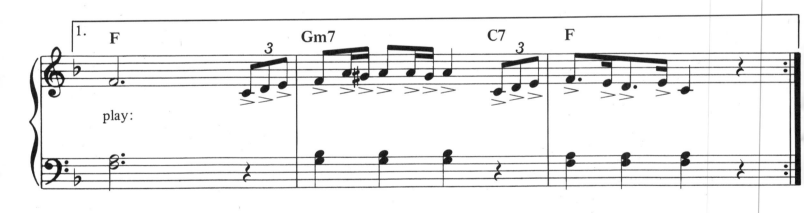

play:

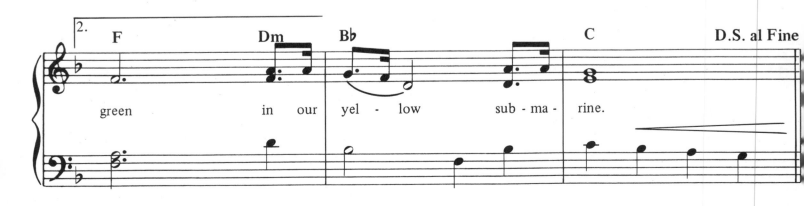

green   in our yel - low sub - ma - rine.

PIANO PLAYING THAT'S FUN & EASY

EASY PIANO BOOKS FROM HAL LEONARD

Irving Berlin's Children's Songbook

13 of his classics, including: Alexander's Ragtime Band • Count Your Blessings Instead of Sheep • Easter Parade • God Bless America • Happy Holiday • White Christmas • and more.
00306047 Easy Piano $7.95

Cartoon Tunes

15 favorite songs from Saturday mornings, including: I'm Popeye the Sailor Man • Jetsons Main Theme • (Meet) The Flintstones • Rocky & Bullwinkle • This Is It • and more.
00222570 Easy Piano $9.95

Children's Favorites For Easy Piano

49 songs children love to play and sing, including: AB-C-DEF-GHI • Bein' Green • C Is for Cookie • Do-Re-Mi • My Favorite Things • Rainbow Connection • Rubber Duckie • Sing • Somebody Come and Play • Won't You Be My Neighbor • and more!
00110014 Easy Piano $10.95

Disney's Silly Songs

Matching easy piano songbook to the album of the same name. 20 humorous songs, including: Baby Bumblebee • Little Bunny Foo Foo • I'm My Own Grandpaw • Three Little Fishies • When I See an Elephant Fly.
00290187 Easy Piano $9.95

Favorite Songs From Jim Henson's Muppets

15 favorite tunes including: Mah-Na-Mah-Na • The Muppet Show Theme • The Rainbow Connection • Rubber Duckie.
00356867 Easy Piano $10.95

The Disney Collection

Over 50 Disney delights, including: The Ballad of Davy Crockett • The Bare Necessities • Bibbidi-Bobbidi-Boo • Candle on the Water • Chim Chim Cher-ee • A Dream Is a Wish Your Heart Makes • Heigh Ho (The Dwarfs' Marching Song) • It's a Small World • Kiss the Girl • The Siamese Cat Song • Someday My Prince Will Come • Supercalifragilisticexpialidocious • Under the Sea • When You Wish upon a Star • Winnie the Pooh • Zip-A-Dee-Doo-Dah • and more.
00222535 Easy Piano $17.95

Disney's Hercules

9 vocal selections, including: The Gospel Truth I, II and III • Go the Distance • Zero to Hero • and more. Includes beautiful full-color art from the movie.
00316020 Easy Piano $14.95

Disney's The Lion King

8 selections, including: Be Prepared • Can You Feel the Love Tonight • Circle of Life • Hakuna Matata • I Just Can't Wait to Be King. Includes both film versions and Elton John solo versions of the songs. Filled with beautiful full-color scenes from the film.
00110029 Easy Piano $14.95

An Illustrated Treasury Of Songs For Children

56 traditional American songs, ballads, folk songs, and nursery rhymes for easy piano. Each song is beautifully complemented with full-color reproductions of famous artworks from the National Gallery of Art, Washington. Songs include: America, The Beautiful • Clementine • The Farmer in the Dell • Hush, Little Baby • I've Been Working on the Railroad • Jingle Bells • Oh, Susanna • On Top of Old Smokey • and more. A wonderful gift idea for a parent or beginning piano student.
00490439 Easy Piano $14.95

Willy Wonka & The Chocolate Factory

What child can resist this sweet collection of 6 songs from their favorite movie, including The Candy Man • Pure Imagination • Oompa Loompa Doompadee-Doo • and more.
00222530 Easy Piano $6.95

FOR MORE INFORMATION, SEE YOUR LOCAL MUSIC DEALER, OR WRITE TO:

HAL•LEONARD®
CORPORATION
7777 W. BLUEMOUND RD. P.O. BOX 13819 MILWAUKEE, WI 53213

0298

The Greatest Songs Ever Written

The Best Ever Collection
Arranged for Easy Piano with Lyrics.

The Best Broadway Songs Ever

Over 65 songs in all! Highlights include: All I Ask of You • All the Things You Are • As Long as He Needs Me • Bess, You Is My Woman • Bewitched • Cabaret • Camelot • Climb Ev'ry Mountain • Comedy Tonight • Don't Cry for Me Argentina • Everything's Coming Up Roses • Getting to Know You • I Could Have Danced All Night • I Dreamed a Dream • If I Were a Rich Man • It Might as Well Be Spring • The Last Night of the World • Love Changes Everything • Memory • My Funny Valentine • Oklahoma! • Ol' Man River • People • Send in the Clowns • Seventy-Six Trombones • Try to Remember • Younger Than Springtime • and many more!
00300178 ....$18.95

The Best Children's Songs Ever

A great collection of 97 songs, including: Alouette • Alphabet Song • The Ballad of Davy Crockett • The Bare Necessities • Be Kind to Your Parents • Beauty and the Beast • Bingo • The Brady Bunch • The Candy Man • A Dream Is a Wish Your Heart Makes • Eensy Weensy Spider • The Farmer in the Dell • Frere Jacques • Friend Like Me • Hakuna Matata • Hello Mudduh, Hello Fadduh! • I Whistle a Happy Tune • I'm Popeye the Sailor Man • Jesus Loves Me • The Muffin Man • My Favorite Things • On Top of Spaghetti • Puff the Magic Dragon • The Rainbow Connection • A Spoonful of Sugar • Take Me Out to the Ball Game • Twinkle, Twinkle Little Star • Winnie the Pooh • and more.
00310360 ....$19.95

The Best Christmas Songs Ever

A collection of 72 of the most-loved songs of the season, including: Auld Lang Syne • Blue Christmas • The Chipmunk Song • The Christmas Song (Chestnuts Roasting on an Open Fire) • Feliz Navidad • Frosty the Snow Man • Grandma Got Run Over by a Reindeer • Happy Holiday • Happy Xmas (War Is Over) • A Holly Jolly Christmas • Home for the Holidays • I Heard the Bells on Christmas Day • I'll Be Home for Christmas • Jingle-Bell Rock • Let It Snow ! Let It Snow ! Let It Snow! • My Favorite Things • Old Toy Trains • Parade of the Wooden Soldiers • Rudolph, The Red-Nosed Reindeer • Santa, Bring Back My Baby (To Me) • Silver Bells • Suzy Snowflake • Toyland • You're All I Want for Christmas • and more.
00364130 ....$18.95

The Best Country Songs Ever

Over 65 songs, featuring: Always on My Mind • Behind Closed Doors • Could I Have This Dance • Crazy • Daddy Sang Bass • Daddy's Hands • Forever and Ever, Amen • Friends in Low Places • God Bless the U.S.A. • Help Me Make It Through the Night • I Fall to Pieces • I Was Country When Country Wasn't Cool • Islands in the Stream • Jambalaya • King of the Road • Love Without End, Amen • Mammas, Don't Let Your Babies Grow Up to Be Cowboys • Paper Roses • Rocky Top • She Thinks I Still Care • Sixteen Tons • Stand by Your Man • Through the Years • To All the Girls I've Loved Before • You Decorated My Life • Your Cheatin' Heart • and more.
00311540 ....$16.95

The Best Love Songs Ever

A collection of 66 favorite love songs, including: Always • And I Love Her • The Anniversary Song • Beautiful in My Eyes • Can You Feel the Love Tonight • Can't Help Falling in Love • (They Long to Be) Close to You • Endless Love • Feelings • Have I Told You Lately • Isn't It Romantic? • Just the Way You Are • Longer • Love Takes Time • Misty • My Funny Valentine • Saving All My Love for You • So in Love • Vision of Love • When I Fall in Love • You Needed Me • Your Song • and more.
00310128 ....$17.95

The Best Movie Songs Ever

Over 70 songs, including: Alfie • Almost Paradise • Beauty and the Beast • Born Free • Circle of Life • Endless Love • Funny Girl • Isn't It Romantic? • It Might As Well Be Spring • Theme from "Jaws" • Theme from "Jurassic Park" • Moon River • Pennies from Heaven • Puttin' on the Ritz • River • Somewhere Out There • Sooner or Later (I Always Get My Man) • Speak Softly, Love • Star Trek® – The Motion Picture • Take My Breath Away • Tears in Heaven • Theme from "Terms of Endearment" • Thanks for the Memory • Unchained Melody • Up Where We Belong • The Way We Were • A Whole New World • and more.
00310141 ....$19.95

The Best Songs Ever

Over 70 must-own classics, including: All I Ask of You • All the Things You Are • Blue Skies • Body and Soul • Candle in the Wind • Crazy • Edelweiss • Endless Love • The Girl from Ipanema • Have I Told You Lately • Imagine • In the Mood • Isn't It Romantic? • Longer • Love Me Tender • Memory • Moonlight in Vermont • My Favorite Things • My Funny Valentine • People • Piano Man • Satin Doll • Save the Best for Last • Send in the Clowns • Somewhere Out There • Strangers in the Night • Tears in Heaven • Unforgettable • The Way We Were • When I Fall in Love • You Needed Me • and more.
00359223 ....$19.95